Pub  *in*

LANCASHIRE

Terry Marsh

• *25 scenic walks including country inns* •

Dalesman

Dalesman Publishing Company
Stable Courtyard, Broughton Hall,
Skipton, North Yorkshire BD23 3AZ

First Edition 1998

Text © Terry Marsh, 1998
Illustrations © Donald Dakeyne
Maps by Jeremy Ashcroft

Cover: The Stork, Conder Green, by Geoff Cowton

A British Library Cataloguing in Publication record
is available for this book

ISBN 1 85568 126 9

Printed by Midas Printing (HK) Ltd

Pub Walks

in

LANCASHIRE

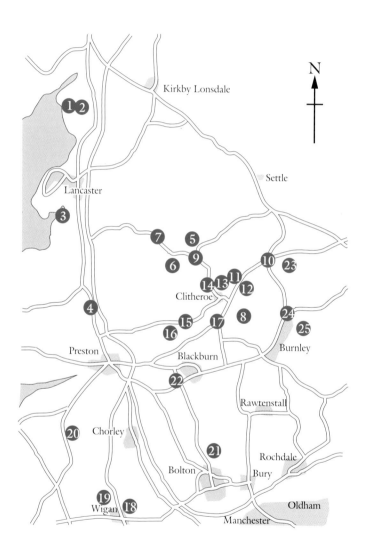

WALKS

INTRODUCTION

In an increasingly modern landscape the place in our heritage of the traditions of the wayside inn is becoming increasingly at risk as many pubs are taken over and 'modernised' by large breweries, and even by Japanese businesses. Sadly, in many cities the familiar pub names are being replaced with modern, nonsensical concoctions, but thankfully the names of many pubs in more rural parts continue to reflect the past, recording history, the fame and deeds of royalty and famous men, local history and a host of unusual local incidents.

Throughout Britain, unlike anywhere else in the world, our pub names and the hand-painted signs that go with them are part of our heritage, and among the treasures of the nation. They must be preserved, and landlords badgered into having faded or damaged signs restored to their former glory. These are miniature works of art, and an important part of the British landscape.

The origin of the pub sign lies with the Romans, who decided that every wine shop should be identified by a bunch of vine leaves, the symbol of Bacchus. As a result, signs incorporating this 'bush' are now commonplace, as in the Ivy Bush, and the Bull and Bush.

In this book, the walks visit a number of pubs having associations with locally important people – the Parkers Arms at Newton, the Ribblesdale Arms at Gisburn, the Assheton Arms, the Bayley Arms and the Crawford Arms. The Eagle and Child likewise commemorates an important local family, though less obviously so, for it refers to the arms of the earls of Derby, the Stanleys.

Of less obvious derivation are pub names like the New

INTRODUCTION

Inn, at Yealand Conyers. Many similarly-named pubs came into being in the 16th century following Elizabeth I's complaint about the lack of suitable places to stay. The Royal Oak, too, has royal connections, alluding to the fact that King Charles II hid in an oak at Boscobel, near Shifnal in Shropshire, in order to escape from Roundhead soldiers after the Battle of Worcester.

The Pendle Witch in Sabden clearly identifies with local legends, though there is little evidence that Sabden was a centre of witchcraft activity; the Orwell at Wigan Pier is a shameless link with Orwell's account of life in Wigan, expressed in *The Road to Wigan Pier*.

Pub names including 'bull' are generally a comment on the importance of the animal in local farming terms, though occasionally they refer to the practice of bull-baiting, a 'sport' made illegal in 1835. Similar associations are linked with inns that bear the name 'Moorcock', as at Blacko, while the Herders Inn at Wycoller, although a change of name, clearly refers to times when the pub was used by drovers and packhorsemen.

The Strawbury Duck at Entwistle used to be called the Station Hotel – no prizes for guessing why. It had long been known locally as the Strawberry, because of the colour of its stonework in certain lights. When the pub became a freehouse, however, the owner, a man called Duxbury, contrived a play on his name and the local name. This unusual name is now part of walkers' folklore around the West Pennine Moors.

All the pubs in this book welcome walkers. They all also

INTRODUCTION

welcome children and, as far as is reasonably acceptable given hygiene regulations, 'Rover' can go along, too. All the landlords have responded to a questionnaire, confirming these points, and also answering questions about the increasingly important need to cater for vegetarians. It is clear, however, that vegetarianism is not fully understood by everyone. Some landlords, for example, believe that it is simply sufficient to provide pizzas, salads or wholemeal bread. Very few, and they have all been sampled by the author, understand about vegetarian cheeses, which are simply those made without animal rennet, and are now widely available.

The opening hours of all pubs are given, along with an indication of whether you can use the pub car park (where there is one), but it is always wise to telephone first if this, and other information, is important.

Finally, since it is unthinkable to condone drinking and driving, all the walks I have given are accessible by public transport. Of particular interest in this regard are the Leisure Link services operated on behalf of the County Council with support from the Countryside Commission. These run on Sundays and Bank Holiday Mondays from May until September, and it is important that they receive as much patronage as possible, especially from walkers, for whom they are intended. You can get a leaflet detailing all these services from any of the County Information Centres. Try using the buses, if you haven't already – give the car a day off – and, like me, you'll discover a whole new dimension to walking in the splendid and invigorating countryside of Lancashire.

PUBLISHER'S NOTE

The information given in this book has been provided in good faith and is intended only as a general guide. Whilst all reasonable efforts have been made to ensure that details were correct at the time of publication, the author and Dalesman Publishing Company Ltd cannot accept any responsibility for inaccuracies. It is the responsibility of individuals undertaking outdoor activities to approach the activity with caution and, especially if inexperienced, to do so under appropriate supervision. They should also carry the appropriate equipment and maps, be properly clothed and have adequate footwear. The sport described in this book is strenuous and individuals should ensure that they are suitably fit before embarking upon it.

SILVERDALE HOTEL

*L**ittle imagination is required to understand why this corner of Lancashire has long been designated an Area of Outstanding Natural Beauty*

DISTANCE:
3$\frac{1}{2}$ miles (6km)
ALLOW:
1$\frac{1}{2}$-2 hours
TERRAIN:
Saltmarsh,
woodland and
country lanes
MAP: OS
Pathfinder 636
PUBLIC
TRANSPORT:
Bus services to
Silverdale. Rail
to Silverdale
station (1 mile
away)
PARKING:
Silverdale Hotel

The Silverdale Hotel along Shore Road has a large beer garden, especially pleasant on warm days. It is a popular hotel both with locals and visitors, and welcomes walkers, children, and dogs (in certain areas only). Bar meals, including many 'specials', are served daily, and include selections suitable for vegetarians. Tel 01524 701206.

From the hotel turn right and walk down Shore Road to reach the foreshore, which quite often floods. Go forward along the saltmarsh (signposted: Lancashire Coastal Way: The Cove), keeping close to projecting rock outcrops, to reach The Cove, conspicuous by a cave low down in a cliff directly ahead.

When you reach The Cove, branch right on a broad track leaving the foreshore, and go through a double gate up Cove Road (signposted: Silverdale Station). At the top of the road, at a T-junction, bear left (signposted: Arnside) and walk along the road for about 200yds/m, and

11

then leave it at a bend, on a footpath signposted for Arnside Tower.

Through an iron gate go forward to reach the edge of a caravan park, where you meet a surfaced lane. Head along the lane, and soon branch left along Elm Grove. Keep following the lane until, at a junction near a waymark, you can leave the caravan site along a path flanked by hazel, hawthorn, holly and bramble. Pass through a gate and keep forward, with Arnside Knott directly ahead, following a path that soon leads to Arnside Tower.

Arnside Tower, thought to have been built in the 15th century, amply testifies to the need in those days to maintain defensive strongholds against marauding Scots. It is a large, oblong pele tower and stands in a splendid position, and though it is now in ruins, part of its corbelled parapet can still be seen, and some idea gained of its former stature.

As you approach the tower go through a gap beside a gate, and bear left following a wall going down to Arnside Tower Farm. On reaching the farm, turn right in front of it, initially on a concrete surface, following a footpath/track signposted to Middlebarrow. The track leads straight to the edge of Middlebarrow Wood, where another gap gives access to the woodland.

Enter the wood on a track (signposted: Middlebarrow and Black Dyke) initially descending. At a junction, keep forward (still signposted for Middlebarrow), and soon walking parallel with the railway. As you leave the woodland, near a quarry, bear left to cross the railway

line, with care. Follow the on-going road which soon bends right, bound for Waterslack.

After about a quarter of a mile, when the opportunity arises, leave this quiet back lane, on the right, to recross the railway line (signposted: Waterslack and Eaves Wood). Go up the lane opposite, passing through a gate to reach Eaves Lee Farm, and on leaving the farm turn right into the National Trust Eaves Wood (signposted) at a gap beside a gate. Take either of the paths that lead into the wood, and shortly turn left at a path junction. When the path forks once more, ignore the left branch through

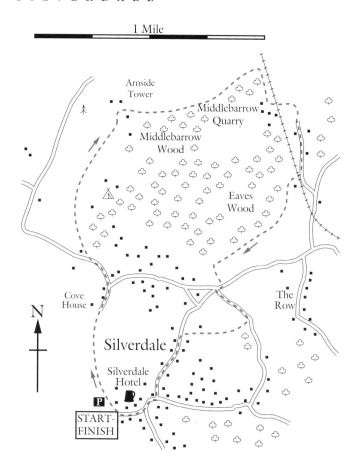

a wide gap in a wall, and bear right instead climbing easily beside a wall. Pass through the wall at an old gateway and then keep forward ignoring turnings right and left.

When the track forks once more, branch left (yellow

waymark), and a short way on leave the main track for a path descending on the left to a wall corner, from where a path, fenced on the left, runs down the edge of a large open pasture to a road. Cross the road and go down Bottoms Lane, and after about 300yds/m leave the road, on the right, at a footpath (signposted: To St John's Church).

Go forward along the field edge, beside a drystone wall. The path goes through a gate in the wall and then continues in the same direction to a stile giving onto a narrow path between and wall and a hedgerow. At the end of the path, turn right on a track (signposted: Emesgate Lane), and follow this out to reach the main road. Turn left up the road towards the village centre.

Go through the village and on the other side turn right on a road signposted to the shore, and follow this back to the Silverdale Hotel.

THE NEW INN

S̲hunning the traditional walks around Leighton, this outing heads east by a roundabout route to the Lancaster Canal

DISTANCE:
6 miles (10km)
ALLOW:
2¹/₂ hours
TERRAIN:
Mostly easy paths, some overgrown. Crossing the A6 requires care
MAPS: OS Pathfinders 636 and 637
PUBLIC TRANSPORT:
Bus services operate through Yealand villages
PARKING:
New Inn car park

This simple early 17th-century ivy-covered stone pub is becoming especially popular for its imaginative blackboard 'specials', as well as its appetising à la carte fare. A simply-furnished beamed bar with a log fire in a big stone fireplace welcomes walkers, while two cottagey dining rooms with black furniture and an attractive kitchen range offer another winter fire. Children and dogs are welcome. Meals are served during all opening hours, which in summer months means all day; vegetarians are well catered for. Tel 01524 732938.

From the New Inn walk up the road, and just past a junction on the left, leave the road, on the right, up steps and through a gap stile on a footpath signposted to Summerhouse Hill. The path strikes slightly left across parkland meadow, passing a group of twelve fence-protected young trees planted in 1993 to commemorate Britain's entry into the European Union.

A signpost in mid-field keeps you on course as you cross a surfaced track. Keep on in the same direction, by now targeting a squeeze stile beside a gate on the far side. Through the stile turn right on a signposted footpath through trees to an old iron gate beyond which the path continues into denser woodland.

As you pass Yealand Manor the path comes to another gate. Go through this and follow the on-going vehicle track (signposted: public footpath to Yealand Redmayne). When the vehicle track bears right to pass through a gate, leave it and keep forward on a broad green track into Cringlebarrow Wood to reach another stile beside a gate.

The on-going path runs beside an attractive ivy- and moss-covered wall. Beyond another gate keep on in the same direction across a large cleared area entirely surrounded by trees, and keep close to the left-hand fenceline. At the far side of the clearing cross a step stile next to a gate to return to the shade of woodland. The path runs down to a five-bar gate and then continues between fences as a broad grassy path with pines and spruce on either side. When the path forks, near a gate, branch left and continue descending, over a low stone step and into a small woodland before coming out onto a road.

Cross the road, bearing right to a gate and a bridleway (signposted: Eight Acre Lane). In the ensuing field bear slightly right to a gate in a fence. Beyond the gate ignore the tempting footpath going off to the right, and go forward alongside a fence on the left to reach another gate. Through this gate turn right on a gravel track along the edge of woodland, and keep forward as you pass through another five-bar gate. The bridleway continues through another gate, crossing the southern edge of White Moss. The on-going path passes some old farm shacks and then becomes a broad vehicle track which very soon bears right. At this point leave the track for a grassy path crossing two stiles in quick succession. As you pass through a five-bar gate go forward and then immediately left over a step stile beside another gate. In the ensuing field follow the right-hand field margin. Ignore a gate on the right and keep forward to another stile near a new barn, and then keep on in the same direction across the next field heading for a metal gate, just beyond which the path (now overgrown) crosses to a step stile beside an ash tree: a nearby gate (if the overgrown section is impassable) gives access to the A6 road.

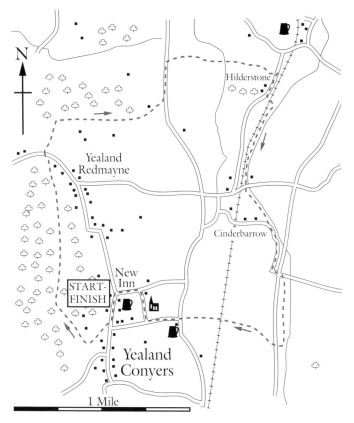

Cross the A6 and turn left up it for 250yds/m, and, opposite Hazel Grove Lodge, turn right on an overgrown bridleway. The bridleway, in spite of being overgrown and in need of walking, continues unerringly between hedgerows/fences to meet a lane near Hilderstone Farm. Turn right along the lane for about 200yds/m and then immediately before the first building on the left leave the road, branching left on a rough-surfaced track that curves round to cross the main west coast railway line by a bridge.

As the on-going track bends right, leave it at a gap stile that gives access to the towpath of the Lancaster Canal. Turn right along the towpath and follow this, past Yealand Road bridge, to approach the M6 motorway. As the canal reaches the motorway it is culverted, and the towpath ends at a gate. Through the gate turn right and follow a track round to a T-junction, there turning left to follow the road over the motorway. On the other side, turn right down a surfaced road just before Saltermire Bridge, to rejoin the towpath about 100yds/m further on.

When you next reach a stone bridge (about 600yds/m from Saltermire Bridge) leave the towpath, branching right through a gate, descending to pass beneath the motorway. On the other side, follow the broad grassy track round to the right as it climbs beside the motorway for a short distance. Thankfully, the track soon leaves the incessant drone of motorway traffic behind, curving left to rise to a gate. Through the gate follow the right-hand field boundary as it curves round and descends to meet a gate beyond which a broad vehicle track leads on beside a wall. The track leads to a bridge across the railway, and then runs on to the A6 once more. Cross the A6 with care, and continue up the lane opposite. After about 300yds/m turn right on a lane that goes past St John's Church, the parish church of Yealand, and at a T-junction turn left to the return to the New Inn.

T he winds that favour the Lune Estuary and the coastal marshes of Cockerham ensure that this visit to an ancient abbey is always a gusty experience

DISTANCE:
8³/₄ miles
(14km)
ALLOW:
3¹/₂-4 hours
TERRAIN:
Easy coastal and
pastureland
walking
MAP: OS
Pathfinder 659
PUBLIC
TRANSPORT:
Buses run
between
Lancaster and
Conder Green
PARKING: The
Stork (but ask
permission first)

Its proximity to the ever-popular Glasson Dock ensures that the Stork at Conder Green receives its share of visitors, especially during the summer months. This unpretentious pub, just to the north of the intestinal twists of the River Conder as it reaches the Lune, is often busy, continuing an inn-keeping tradition on this site that has lasted for more than 300 years. It welcomes walkers at all times of the year. Children and dogs are also welcome. Bar meals, which include three or four choices specifically for vegetarians, are served Monday-Friday from 12 noon to 2.30pm and 6.30pm until 9.00pm; Saturday from 12 noon to 2.30pm and 6.00pm until 9.30pm; Sunday 12 noon until 9.00pm.

Close by the Stork, an old railway line, which saw service from 1883 until 1964, links Lancaster and Glasson Dock. To reach it go along the surfaced lane in front of the Stork, and as you approach the entrance to a picnic site, built in an

old cutting, turn left onto the railway trackbed
(signposted: Lancashire Coastal Way), which finally
reaches Glasson beside the road and the Victoria Inn.

*No longer of key maritime importance, Glasson Dock is still
active as a marina and safe haven for leisure craft. It was
developed to accommodate sea-going vessels prevented by the
silting up of the River Lune from reaching the heart of
Lancaster. In 1826 the Lancaster Canal was extended to
Glasson, allowing goods to travel the canal network
between Kendal, Lancaster, Preston and further south.*

Having used the trackbed to reach Glasson, cross the
road towards the Glasson Basin and go left across a
swing bridge. Keep ahead, ascending Tithebarn Hill, and
at the top bear left and follow the road a short way
further until at a sharp left bend you can turn right into
Marsh Lane (signposted: Bridleway), and go past a
caravan site to open pastureland at a gate. A short stretch
of muddy walking follows as the track crosses a field.
Keep ahead beside a line of hawthorns and then bear left
with the track as it moves towards a gate, beyond which
the track runs up to Crook Farm overlooking the Lune.
On reaching the farm go left along the Lancashire
Coastal Way, following a surfaced drive, and stay with
this shoreline-hugging track, past the end of Slack Lane
and its nearby car park, to reach Cockersand Abbey.

*Beginning as a hermitage in about 1180, Cockersand
became an abbey of the Premonstratensian Order in 1190.
In 1539 the abbot and 22 canons surrendered it to the
King's Commissioners, and it has lain in ruins since. This
site was the hermitage of Hugh Garth, whose reputation
led to the establishment here of a hospital for lepers, and*

ten years later the priory.

A short detour is needed to visit the abbey ruins, but having done so stroll across coastal turf back to the edge of the estuary. Follow this now to Bank Houses.

As you approach Bank Houses, leave the grassy path and drop below a wall onto a concrete walkway that leads past ruined buildings to a surfaced lane at a gate. Keep ahead (east), with a caravan park on your left, following a narrow path, and soon reach Bank End Farm.

Keep on past Bank End Farm, beyond which a surfaced lane runs east. An adjoining embankment (not a right of way) provides a more elevated view of coastal pastures that, like much of this walk, often provide a wealth of ornithological interest. Stay with the lane, to reach the village of Hillam. Keep on through the village to a footpath about 300yds/m beyond the village on the right. Turn right, through a gate onto a broad cart track, and when the track shortly bends left, go ahead through

23

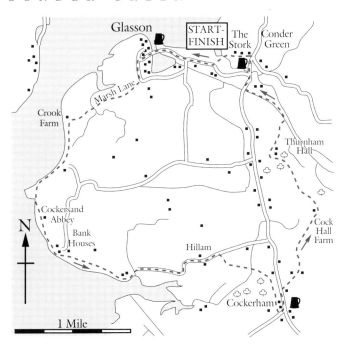

another gate, following a field boundary with a drainage ditch and fence on the left. This guides you to a footbridge over a stream, beyond which you aim for Ware Cottage ahead which is preceded by a low step stile.

Cross in front of the cottage to reach its access lane from the A588 (though there may in future be some slight diversion here as the way past the cottage becomes better defined). As the access bends left, go forward over two stiles, and then half left to another stile in a top field corner giving into a builder's compound. Press on, between buildings to reach a lane descending into the village of Cockerham.

On reaching Cockerham, go left along the A588 as far as the access, on the right, to Batty Hill Farm. Keep ahead through the farm buildings, then curve left to descend a sunken trackway, flanked by sycamore trees. Go on through a gate and ahead along a muddy cart track. This brings you to a series of gates, along a hedgerowed lane, until you reach a waymark sending you left into a wide pasture. Head across the pasture, towards Cock Hall Farm. Keep a pond to your right, and cross a footbridge, then head for the buildings of Cock Hall Farm ahead.

Waymarks steer you between the farm buildings, and out to its access lane, which leads to the village of Thurnham. Go past the church, which dates from 1785, and follow the track through mixed woodland until you can turn right in front of Thurnham Hall Country Club. Go past the hall, down a broad track, and after a group of derelict farm buildings, bear right. A short way on look for a waymark on an ash tree on the left, near an old gateway. Go left here through the obsolete gateway, and then ahead across a pasture into an overgrown lane that is often wet and muddy, to reach a ladder stile.

Over the stile bear right to Bailey Bridge on the Glasson Branch of the Lancaster Canal. Cross the bridge, but do not go through the gate on the other side. Instead, squeeze through a narrow stile on the left and descend rough steps to the canal towpath.

The canal towpath now heads back to Glasson Dock, passing The Millers pub, formerly Thurnham Mill. When you reach Conder Green road (A588) leave the towpath and turn right to follow the road back to the Stork.

OWD NELL'S TAVERN

B I L S B O R R O W

A *pleasant stroll beside the Lancaster Canal and the River Brock awaits visitors to this corner of Lancashire*

DISTANCE:
4 miles (6.5km)
ALLOW:
1¹/₂-2 hours
MAPS: OS
Pathfinder 668
and 679
TERRAIN:
Good paths
beside canal and
river, and across
fields; some
road walking
PUBLIC
TRANSPORT:
Bus services
operate along
the nearby A6
PARKING:
Cricket pavilion
car park at the
rear of Guy's
Thatched
Hamlet

Owd Nell's Tavern is part of a thriving little complex called Guy's Thatched Hamlet which has transformed a neglected stretch of the Lancaster Canal. There is a hotel with indoor pool and gym, and various craft and tea shops. This busy pub still maintains a relaxing, rustic feel, with a mix of brocaded banquettes, stable-stall seating, and library chairs, high pitched rafters and low beams (and flagstones) by the bar counter; a couple of areas are non-smoking. Children are made especially welcome, as are dogs (under control). There are colourful seats out on the terrace, part of which is covered by a thatched roof. There is a good selection of pub grub, and vegetarians are catered for. Bar food from 10.30am to 10.00pm; reservations advised at weekends and bank holidays. Tel 01995 640010.

From the cricket pavilion car park walk back towards the main group of buildings, crossing a small stream

(Bacchus Brook), and turn left to pass through School House Square and reach the canal towpath. The name commemorates School House Farm which used to stand on the site occupied by Owd Nell's.

Turn left along the towpath, and soon pass beneath a single arch bridge. There is no escape from the sound of traffic on this walk, but the canal soon tries to steer you away as it swings westwards to reach Brock Aqueduct. The aqueduct, first used in 1797, is a single span, 60 feet long, and carrying the canal 22 feet above the River Brock; the engineer was John Rennie.

Keep on along the towpath until at Bridge 47, having passed beneath it, you can go up a flight of steps to reach the A6. Now turn left and walk beside the road towards Preston, taking great care, especially if you have children with you. On the right you pass the Green Man pub, formerly a toll house on the turnpike from London to the north. A short way further on you can leave this busy road at a footpath signpost. Go left here to reach a gate at the main north-south railway line. Care is again called for as you cross the line, to continue along a surfaced pathway between hedgerows. This soon leads to the River Brock where the path swings left to head upstream and pass beneath the M6.

Keep on beyond the motorway to reach an aluminium bridge spanning the river, and cross it. On the other side, bear right to pass the ruins of the Matshead Paper Mill. The path crosses a cobbled yard beside a cottage, and goes through a gap to the left of a garage. Having done so, go forward to a high fence at the corner of which there is a gate. Through the gate you enter a grassed area that adjoins more houses. Walk ahead to a stile over a low fence, and go across the field beyond to another stile.

Over the stile follow the field margin, with a hedgerow on your right. Ignore a double metal gate in the hedge, instead keeping ahead around the field boundary to a metal gate in an adjacent fence. Beyond this the path runs on to cross a stream, Bull Brook, by a wooden footbridge. Now a concrete farm access takes you on to reach Bilsborrow Hall Farm. Go through the farm buildings, and walk out to reach a road. As you reach the road turn right and walk along the verge to recross the motorway, and keep on past the Bilsborrow Wesleyan Sunday School, next to which stands the octagonal Bilsborrow Methodist Chapel in which, it is said, earthenware pots were once made.

As you continue so you cross the railway line, this time

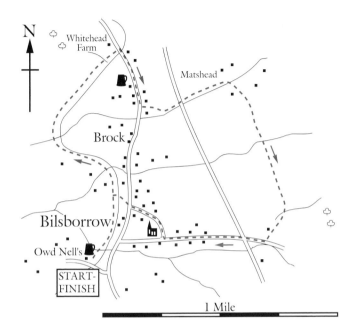

on a road bridge, and immediately turn right into Church
Lane, to pass St Hilda's Church. The church was built in
1926-7 by the architects Austin and Paley from the estate
of Jane Salisbury of Myerscough Hall, who died crossing
the railway at Brock Station: it was consecrated in 1927.

By following Church Lane you eventually return to the
A6. Turn right, and then immediately cross the road at an
island. Walk along the far side to signposted Myerscough
Hall Drive, and here turn left, soon recrossing the
Lancaster Canal. Over the canal bridge, turn left down
steps to regain the towpath, and then retrace your steps
to Owd Nell's.

HARK TO BOUNTY

S L A I D B U R N

A fine, extended walk around Stocks Reservoir and adjoining pastures

DISTANCE:
9 miles
(14.5km)
ALLOW:
4-5 hours
TERRAIN:
Tracks and
paths, with one
(usually) easy
river crossing
MAP:
OS OLM 41
PUBLIC
TRANSPORT:
Buses run to
Slaidburn, plus
the Bowland
Rambler and
Bowland
Pathfinder (May
to September)
PARKING:
Hark to Bounty
(space limited,
so ask
permission first)

Formerly known as 'The Dog', the Hark to Bounty Inn dates from the 13th century, and contains a first-floor courtroom still in use until 1937. Walkers and children are welcome at the Hark to Bounty; dogs, too, but not when food is being served. Bar meals, which include Children's Specials and a selection of meals for vegetarians are served Monday to Thursday 12 noon to 2.00pm and 6.30pm to 9.00pm; Friday and Saturday from 12 noon to 2.00pm and 6.30pm to 9.30pm; and Sunday 12 noon to 3.00pm, and 5.30pm to 8.00pm. Tel 01200 446246.

Walk to the war memorial and turn left onto the lane beside it. Once across Croasdale Brook, go right, into a field and across to a wall on the far side. The wall guides you to a track that takes you to cross the River Hodder, beyond which you continue to Hammerton Hall.

Keep on to farm buildings and branch right to three gates. Choose that on the left, and follow a line of

waymarks past Black House and out along the access road towards St James's Church. Turn left up the road to the Gisburn Forest car park.

Go through the car park onto a number of waymarked trails (red and white), and follow these until you discover a yellow waymark (about ten minutes or so), which should be ignored. Keep straight on to reach a clearing. Branch left and a few more minutes will bring you out of the forest, to cross Hasgill Beck.

A good track leads to the ruins of New House, shortly before which turn left through a gate, soon reaching a walled lane. Turn left and in a minute or so go right, through a gate into a field. Turn right and follow a wall to a gate beyond which a green track leads to a ford at

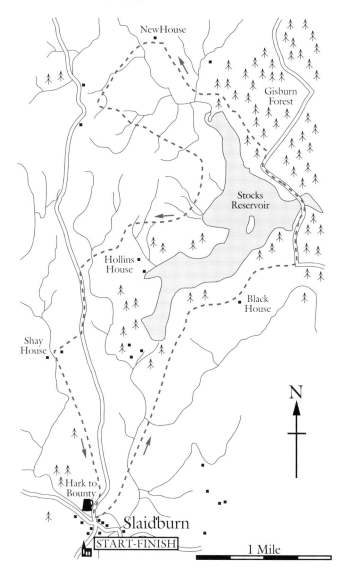

the River Hodder. (If you don't like the thought of crossing the river (seldom a problem), the map shows an alternative loop up towards Catlow, crossing the river at Lock Bridge (GR.713584), rejoining the original line a short distance south of Kenibus, at a road corner.)

Once across the ford cross a field to a gate and on to Collyholme. Go through a large gap in a wall on the left then follow a stream and cross a couple of stiles. This brings you to a wide green track and a gate. Beyond the gate, leave the track and bear right. Another green track appears, and turns out to be a former railway once used to bring stone from a quarry. Follow the track for one-and-a-half miles until it starts to pass a hollow, where a footpath sign marks the point at which to leave it.

Go uphill, near woodland, past a barn ruin to another barn. Go past the ruins, and in a hollow you find a clear path that leads you over a shoulder, across a stream by a simple bridge, then bearing left to woodland. Cross a stile, bearing half left to a waymark, then going down the field to the track leading to Hollins House.

Turn right along the track, to reach the road. Go left down the road as far as the track to Shay House, and here turn right to approach Croasdale Brook. Just before the brook, go left over a stile into a field, the first of many (with stiles) that lead you in much the same direction always back towards the road, which you meet just a short way out of Slaidburn.

Turn right, continuing down to cross Croasdale Beck on the edge of Slaidburn, and then go left as you enter the village to return to the Hark to Bounty.

INN AT WHITEWELL

F O R E S T   O F   B O W L A N D

Green pastures and riverside rambling in a delightful corner of Bowland

DISTANCE:
7 miles (11 km)
ALLOW:
3-3½ hours
MAP:
OS OLM 41
TERRAIN:
Pathless green pastures, quiet lanes. Some road walking
PUBLIC TRANSPORT:
Bus services to Whitewell from Clitheroe and Settle, plus the Ribble Valley Rambler and Bowland Pathfinder
PARKING: The Inn at Whitewell (ask permission)

Tremendously popular and beautifully set in the Hodder valley, the Inn at Whitewell is surrounded by rolling, wooded hills, high moors, and bright green pastures that in early spring host a cacophony of bleating appeals from new-born lambs. The Inn has the air of a friendly country house, its bar fitted with antique settles, gateleg tables, clocks, and cricketing and sporting prints. Its spaciousness ensures that in spite of its popularity, there is almost always a quiet spot in which to relax. Walkers are very welcome, though it would be appreciated if muddy boots could be left at the door. Bar meals served all year round (except Christmas Day) from 12 noon to 2.00pm and from 7.30pm to 9.30pm. Vegetarians are catered for. Children, too, are welcome, as are dogs. Tel 01200 448222.

Start by walking up the lane opposite the Inn, but after about 80yds/m leave it at a signposted footpath on the right, reached by a

flight of stone steps and a gate. Walk forward to go
through the remains of a gate at the end of a dilapidated
wall and head for the house at Seed Hill Farm.
Immediately in front of the farm you intercept a broad
track. Turn right, along this, and follow its course as it
sweeps across a hillside eventually to reach a wall.

*Behind and to the right, as you rise above the valley, you
can see across the Hodder farmlands to the wide gorge that
contains the River Dunsop.*

At the wall go through the left-hand of two gates and
immediately turn right beside another wall to reach a
couple of wrought-iron gates. Beyond the gates go
forward along a fenceline to a stile, and then keep on in
the same direction beside a fence to reach a wall and
another gate. Through the gate, keep ahead on a broad
green path beside a fence. The track eventually runs on to

reach a duplicate pair of wrought-iron gates, after which go half right across a pathless pasture towards a junction between a road wall on the right and another fence. There go through a gate and rejoin the road about 30yds/m further on.

Turn left along the road for 50yds/m, crossing the top edge of a mixed plantation, and leaving the road at a footpath sign on the right, at a stile. Go forward into the field, aiming for the dark left edge of a plantation ahead, and passing beneath power lines on the way. There is a faint green track on the ground. When you reach an isolated and gnarled hawthorn, all that remains of a former hedgerow no doubt of some antiquity, keep forward in the same direction with a low embankment on your left. This, too, may mark the line of an ancient hedgerow, one of many old field boundaries that are fast disappearing from the British countryside.

The route approaches woodland ahead. Do not enter it, but keep to its outside edge, and go down to a gate that soon appears.

Away from the modicum of civilisation that Whitewell represents, the farmlands are populated by a wide range of birds from buzzards to oystercatchers, treecreepers, grey wagtails, curlews, partridges and lapwings. There are numerous rabbits about, too, along with the occasional hare.

Cross a stile beside the gate, beyond which the River Hodder puts in an appearance down to your right. Go slightly left along the course of another cleared hedgerow.

The path ambles on in a most agreeable fashion, the air of

*peace punctuated at times by the sound of woodpeckers
among the trees across the river. An occasional hawthorn
confirms that the route is still following the line of an
ancient field boundary.*

At the end of the field you cross an in-flowing stream at a
ford, and a short way on go through two gates about
50yds/m apart. After the second gate climb onto a slight
rise just ahead, and then go forward to yet another gate.
Keep ahead to a tree-lined gully at the foot of which a
rough farm track materialises. Cross the gully and climb
the other side, bearing slightly left to reach and follow an
ascending hollow way that rises to meet a gate at a
rough-surfaced farm access.

On reaching the access, turn right, and when the track
comes down to a barn near the river, bear right to
approach a farm. As you draw level with the farm, go
right to cross the river on stepping stones.

The River Hodder is quite wide at this point, but not
especially deep, and rarely do the stepping stones get
covered. But don't take any risks if the river level is
higher than usual, simply about turn and retrace your
steps to Whitewell, a rather more appealing prospect than
might be supposed.

On the other side cross a stile and walk forward to a
footbridge spanning Greystoneley Brook near Wardsley
Farm. Over the bridge, turn left along a surfaced lane,
following this round to a road junction, and there turn
right (signposted to Chipping). Walk along the lane for a
quarter of a mile, with a fine view of the Bowland Fells
ahead. The adjacent hawthorn hedgerow in spring

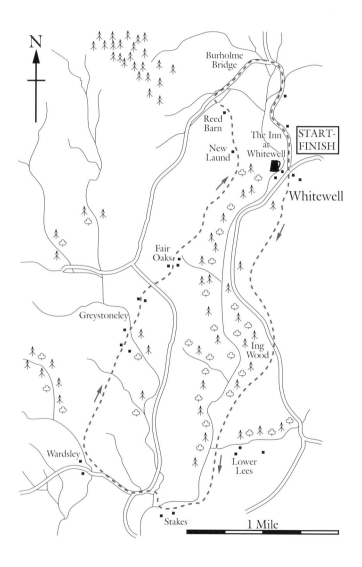

shelters dog's mercury, cowslip, lesser celandine, and cuckoo pint, the latter also known as lords and ladies.

Just before reaching a cottage, leave the road on the right, along a bridleway that leads to Lower Greystoneley Farm. Keep on past the farmhouse, and go forward between farm buildings to reach a track descending into woodland. Either ford the stream at the bottom of the track, or use the nearby footbridge, and then keep on up a rough-surfaced track that rises steadily to Higher Greystoneley Farm. Pass between the farm buildings and follow the farm access out to reach a lane.

On reaching the lane turn right for 30yds/m, and then leave it on the left at a signposted footpath over a stile. Another stile quickly follows giving access to a large pasture. In the pasture bear half right heading for the buildings of Fair Oak Farm that can just be seen. Enter the farmyard by a stile at a wooden fence corner, and walk forward, then left and right between outbuildings to reach the end of a surfaced access lane.

Turn left here, go past a house on the right, and just before the next house (this time on the left), descend right on a rough track that goes through a dip, rising on the other side as a stony track. This meanders onwards, heading for the mound of New Laund Hill. When the track runs out into an open field, follow a fenceline round to the left, and then keep on beside a dilapidated wall to a ladder stile.

Over the stile ascend a green track ahead, cutting slightly right across the hillside. As the path reaches its highest point the village of Whitewell re-appears in the valley below, as does Burholme Bridge to the left, by means of which the return to Whitewell is effected.

Follow the descending path to a gate, and walk forward beyond the gate into a descending valley, using the bridge as a target. The route keeps on to reach a stony track at the rear of New Laund Farm. Go into the farmyard, and turn left, leaving along its access track. This passes Reed Barn Farm before finally reaching a lane. Turn right along the lane, shortly to cross Burholme Bridge from where the road leads back to Whitewell.

There is no footpath along much of this stretch of road, so care is needed at all times. Along the way a concessionary path, off the road and along a field margin, relieves some of the road hazard, but finally rejoins the road opposite Higher Whitewell Farm. A quarter of a mile of road walking then remains.

The rustic charms of Chipping form a springboard for the exploration of the high fells that gather above the village

DISTANCE:
5 miles (8km)
ALLOW:
3-4 hours
TERRAIN: Hill paths and farm tracks; not suitable for misty conditions
MAP:
OS OLM 41
PUBLIC TRANSPORT:
Buses run to Chipping, plus the Bowland Wanderer during summer months
PARKING:
Village centre car park, opposite church

The Sun Inn is a popular pub in the centre of Chipping and a most welcome place on a hot summer day. Walkers are especially welcome, as are children, and there is a small beer garden at the rear of the pub. Bar meals are served from 12 noon to 6.00pm, though there is no provision for vegetarians. Tel 01995 61206.

Chipping is a delightful concoction of narrow streets and bright cottages, almshouses and venerable buildings, pubs and an interesting church. All this highlights that Chipping, a name that means a market, was once a welcome halt on the cross-country routes that braid the fells of Bowland Forest. In 1992, Chipping was Winner in the Champion Class of the Best Kept Village Competition, and in 1995 won in the Champion Village Class.

This circular walk is possible only as a result of the efforts of Lancashire County Council's Countryside Service in negotiating open access areas and developing a series of concessionary pathways with North West Water. The consequence is to open up an area that for years was closed to walkers,

*but there is a small price to pay if you are a dog owner,
because dogs are not allowed under any circumstances. The
walk entails 1,115ft (350m) of height gain.*

Leave the car park heading towards the church and turn
left up the lane, and just over 200yds/m further on
branch right passing the chair works, a traditional
industry in Chipping. When you reach a mill pond, the
path to Burnslack begins along the driveway to a house
on the right, though it is easy to miss.

Having found it, go steeply up-field, and along a
fenceline to a stile, keeping above a wooded clough to a

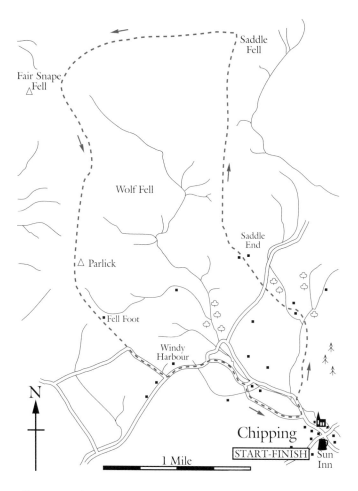

Saddle
Fell

Fair Snape
Fell
△

Wolf Fell

△ Parlick

Saddle
End

Fell Foot

Windy
Harbour

N

Chipping

START-FINISH

Sun
Inn

1 Mile

stile. From the stile a path strikes through the woodland
to a footbridge. Cross it and head up to Windy Hill
Farm, there bearing left onto its access road, following
this out to a surfaced lane.

Cross the land and go along the access past Saddle End
Farm to a broad track rising onto Saddle Fell. Soon you
reach the edge of an Access Area. Once in the Area, the
track continues to rise, divides, re-joins, but goes ever
upwards. There is slightly easier going to the right-hand
side of Saddle Fell, and this links in to a better defined
track higher up. Keep going in a northerly direction and
you will eventually intersect the fence across the
watershed. Totridge lies to the right, and Fair Snape Fell
to your left.

Turn left and follow a concessionary pathway to the
summit of Fair Snape Fell, which is marked by a large
cairn.

On Fair Snape Fell, cross the nearby fence by a stile, and
follow the on-going fence/wall first in a south-westerly
direction, then east of south and downhill before
changing direction slightly once more to reach the green
dome of Parlick.

From the top of Parlick you follow an obvious path
down to the cottage at Fell Foot. From Fell Foot, walk
down a surfaced lane to a junction. Keep ahead to a
T-junction at Fish House Lane. Keep right at the next
junction and then pursue pleasant lanes all the way back
to Chipping; but do take care against traffic.

THE PENDLE WITCH

*T*he grassy expanse of Spence Moor is just one of numerous 'moors' that comprise Pendle Hill, that famous Lancashire landmark

DISTANCE:
5 miles (8km)
ALLOW:
3 hours
TERRAIN:
Moorland paths, farm lanes and tracks
MAPS:
OS OLM 21
PUBLIC TRANSPORT:
Buses to Sabden, plus the summertime Pendle Witch Hopper
PARKING: The Pendle Witch (but ask permission first)

In an area steeped in tales of witchcraft it is not surprising to find at least one pub that keeps the legends alive. The Pendle Witch, on Whalley Road, is a popular pub locally, and especially welcomes walkers. Children, too, are welcome (there's an outdoor play area for them), but no dogs, please. Bar meals, including selections for vegetarians, are served seven days a week from 12 noon to 5.00pm. Tel 01282 771579.

During the 18th century Sabden was a busy village, mainly as a staging post for the packhorse trains that crossed between the Lancashire and Yorkshire valleys. But its place along an ancient cross-country route pre-dates Norman times. In spite of its associations with witchcraft, however, there is little evidence that it was ever a focus of such attention. This walk involves 1,015ft (310m) of ascent.

From the pub, walk up towards the church of St. Nicholas. On reaching its entrance, go left up a lane to Badger Wells Cottages. Keep on

45

round bends to a junction at Cockshotts Farm, and here go left to cross Churn Clough, following the on-going lane as it climbs to the terraced Badger Wells Cottages.

As you approach the cottages, go to their right to access a sunken pathway, ascending easily to a gate. Beyond, a green path leads to another gate at which you pursue a course parallel with Badger Wells Water. Continue with the path as it eases upwards to reach the open fellside at a wall and gate. When the on-going path meets an east-west track, turn right along it crossing the top end of a field before continuing once more above the intake wall.

A short way on the rocky outcrop of Deerstones appears. As it does, ignore a branching track on the left, and press on to cross a tree-lined clough. Once across the clough the track rises and degenerates into a narrow path as it approaches a larch plantation.

Follow the boundary of the plantation and descend to cross a stream. Ignore a stile into the plantation, and rise left on a peaty path to tackle the brackeny hillside below Deerstones. At the top edge of the plantation keep ahead, rising on a clear path that soon escapes the bracken and peat to pursue a grassy course, gradually approaching and then swinging round above the rocks of Deerstones.

As the path rises above Deerstones, so it meets a path branching left to a wall. Ignore this, and stroll on to the pathless, tussocky top of Deerstones before crossing to reach the wall at a stile, beyond which a path leads on to the higher ground of Spence Moor, finally bringing Pendle Hill into view beyond the ravine of Ogden Clough. The path continues south-east and descends

obliquely to meet a wall at a stile. Across the wall a path trails down through marshy moorland. At a gate at the bottom of the hill pasture the main path branches left, for Newchurch-in-Pendle. Ignore this, and keep ahead, descending roughly parallel with a steep-sided gully to the ruins of an old barn.

Pass the ruin and go through a former gateway, immediately doubling back to reach a dilapidated wall running down to the top edge of Cock Clough Plantation. Keep to the outside of the plantation, on a descending sunken pathway, to the outskirts of Sabden Fold Farm, and going down past the farm to a surfaced lane. There, turn right, to go in front of the farm.

Follow the lane for a short distance, and go right with it past Lower Lane Farm, where the surfaced lane

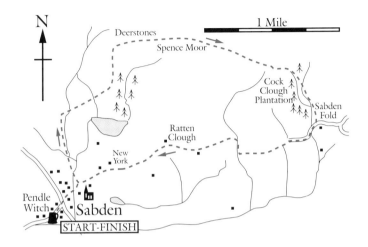

degenerates to a cobbled track flanked by hawthorn and holly. The track continues to Wood House Farm, fords a stream and swings right to the ruins of Stainscomb, once a fine Tudor farmstead with mullioned windows. As Stainscomb is reached, the track swings up and left to begin an easy and level promenade, bound for the next farm, Ratten Clough.

Ahead now the steeple of Sabden church reappears as the farm track leads on to Ratten Clough. Go through the farmyard and then follow a surfaced lane to New York Farm, from where a narrow hedgerowed lane runs down to rejoin the outward route at Cockshotts Farm. Turn left, and retrace your steps to the village.

PARKERS ARMS HOTEL

A visit to Slaidburn along the Hodder, and a tour of Pain Hill, await

DISTANCE:
4¹/₄ miles (7km)
ALLOW:
2-2¹/₂ hours
TERRAIN:
Grassy paths, trackless fields and lanes
MAP:
OS OLM 41
PUBLIC TRANSPORT:
Regular buses run through Newton, including the Morecambe Bay Rambler, the Bowland Pathfinder and Rambler
PARKING:
Limited. £5 at Parkers Arms, redeemable against food and drink

The Parkers Arms is popular with walkers to this corner of the Forest of Bowland, and the redeemable parking charge is a reasonable safeguard against indiscriminate use of its car park. Walkers are always welcome, as are children (there is an animal/wildlife garden), but dogs must be kept to the beer garden. Bar meals, which include a number of hot and cold options for vegetarians, are served from Monday to Friday from 12 noon to 2.30pm and 6.00pm to 9.00pm, continuous from 12 noon to 9.00pm from June to September and throughout the year on Saturdays and Sundays. Tel 01200 446236.

From the Parkers Arms turn right and go down the lane to Newton Bridge, which spans the River Hodder. On reaching the bridge, don't cross it, but leave the lane on a signposted footpath through a gated gap. Cross a small field to another gate that gives onto a footpath running through riverside scrub, and leads to a small footbridge. Beyond

49

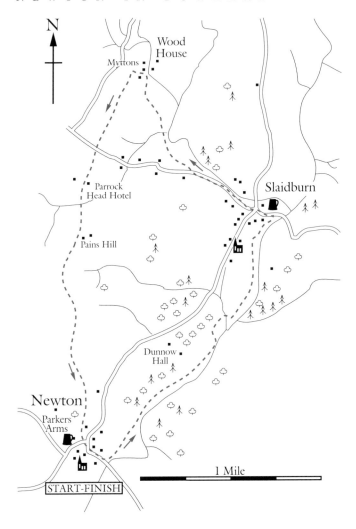

the bridge go forward on a grassy path beside a moss-covered wall to another gated gap, and then in the next field turn left beside a wall, and continue in the same direction alongside a fence.

Having abandoned the river for a while, the path now rejoins it at a step stile. Over the stile continue on the obvious path along the base of woodland to an iron kissing gate, beyond which follow the course of the river, upstream, to a footbridge about 300yds/m distant, and then keep on along a riverside path with Dunnow Hall set against woodland to the left.

Dunnow Hall was built in the 1830s by the Wilkinson family, ancestors of the Squire of Slaidburn, John Norgrave King-Wilkinson, and it stands on the site of a 17th-century house.

When the riverside path reaches a North West Water compound, detour around it to rejoin the path by means of a step stile onto a permissive path.

The path keeps on to a wooden kissing gate on the outskirts of Slaidburn, and continues through riverside woodland into the village. Turn left at the Methodist church and go up into the village.

In the village centre, keep forward, past the Hark to Bounty Inn, and follow the lane for about 300yds/m and then branch right on a footpath signposted for Woodhouse, descending into woodland adjoining Croasdale Brook. When the path comes out of the woodland, and in so doing leaving the brook for a moment, keep forward beside a fence to a step stile, then keeping on in the same direction, descending to a ladder stile close by a loop in Croasdale Brook's meandering course.

Over the stile, keep beside the brook to a through stile. Immediately beyond cross a narrow, slab footbridge and then strike across the ensuing field on a narrow grassy trod to a gate at a wall corner. Through the gate keep forward beside a wall, and as you approach Wood House, bear right with the wall as it turns through 90 degrees, and go down a broad grassy track that leads to Myttons Farm Crafts Shop.

Turn left in front of the shop. Ignore a waymarked footpath going off to the right, but stay along the farm access for 130yds/m, and at a large barn, go left over a step stile towards a metal gate. Just to the left of the gate, cross a right-angled through stile at a wall corner, and then continue on a green path beside a wall on your right. Keep following the wall until you meet another through stile, and in the next field go forward following the line of an old hawthorn hedgerow, and later cross another through stile, just to the left of a field gate. Then go forward, slightly left, across the ensuing field to a step stile, giving onto a surfaced lane, almost opposite the entrance to Parrock Head Farmhouse Hotel and Restaurant.

Cross the road and go down the access to the hotel, and across its car park to a field gate at the rear. Beyond the gate the onward route is pathless and not immediately obvious. Ahead, and slightly right, in the distance stands Pain Hill Farm; this is your objective – if visibility is poor, use a compass and strike a course just west of south. To continue, go downhill from the gate (ignore a tempting pathway slanting left down-field), heading for the farm. This line, there is no footpath, brings you to a

through stile in a wall, beyond which lies Eller Beck, crossed by a footbridge. Then go up the following field towards Pain Hill Farm, aiming for the right-hand edge of the buildings. There a through stile at a wall corner gives access to a broad track.

Turn right for a few strides and then go left around a barn, and then along a vehicle track beside a wall and small copse to a five-bar gate and an adjacent through stile. In the next field, leave the on-going vehicle track and bear left towards a wall, and just past a wall junction over the wall, on the left, cross a through stile.

From this position two woodland copses can be seen on the horizon. Aim for the left-hand edge of the right-hand copse, and there you will find a step stile at a fence corner. Over the stile, go half-right across rough ground, moving away from the copse. When a wall and fence come into view, head for the point where they meet, and there cross a step stile. Over the stile go down-field beside a wall, and soon the grey-topped village of Newton comes into view in the valley below.

Lower down you go through a gate at a wall/fence junction, and then bear half-left down the ensuing field (no path), to a step stile beside a metal gate (waymarks at the gate relate to a different path). Over the stile go down to the bottom left-hand corner of the field. There is an improving path as you go, which becomes a track and leads you on across fields and through hedgerow gaps and gates eventually to reach the rear garden of Hare and Hounds Cottage. Cross a gravelled area, half-left, and go through an open gateway to the front of the cottage (where waymarks confirm that you have done the right thing). Bear left to go down to the village road. Cross the road and go down the Clitheroe road, past the Old Reading Room to return to the Parkers Arms Hotel.

RIBBLESDALE ARMS

&xplore rolling pastures and stream-side ways on this tour of the countryside around Gisburn

DISTANCE:
6¹/₂ miles
(10km)
ALLOW:
2¹/₂-3 hours
TERRAIN:
Lanes, field
paths and tracks,
mostly across
farmland
MAP:
OS OLM 41
PUBLIC
TRANSPORT:
Good bus
services run
through Gisburn
PARKING: The
Ribblesdale
Arms

Gisburn has been an important market town since the 17th century, and the Ribblesdale Arms was very much a part of the scene, as it is today. Walkers are welcome here, as are children and dogs. Bar meals are served daily, and include at least three dishes suitable for vegetarians. Tel 01200 445149.

From the Ribblesdale Arms turn right and walk along the A59 as far as the cattle market, and there turn right into Mill Lane. Follow Mill Lane as first it crosses the railway line and then descends through Coppice Wood to meet the River Ribble at Gisburn Bridge.

As you reach the bridge, but before crossing it, turn right around a building onto a bridleway, a roughly-surfaced lane, following this into sparse woodland. Follow the on-going track past buildings into Gisburne Park, former home to the lords of Ribblesdale. Bear right across a cattle grid, and just beyond, as the track forks, branch left and keep on to a gate. Beyond the gate three possibilities await. Take the middle one, descending on a rough track into woodland and crossing Stock Beck at a hump-backed bridge, just beyond which, keep to the left of a large house, and follow a rising, stony track to the top edge of the woodland at old gate pillars. Keep forward along the ensuing vehicle track, which leads out to meet the A682. Cross this with care to a gate opposite.

In the ensuing pasture go forward to meet a stream. Keep the stream on your right, but as it makes a pronounced bend to the left you can cross it at the second of two culverted sections. Strike half left across the pasture beyond heading for the abutments of a railway bridge.

Go under the railway bridge and about 30yds/m further on go left through a gate. In the ensuing field move

roughly parallel with the fence for about 100yds/m then pick up a narrow grassy path heading across the field to a gate on the far side, now with Painley Farm in view.

Go through the gate and on towards the farm, passing through more gates to reach the farm access. Head along this, ignoring a turning to the left. Keep on along the access to meet a lane a short distance west of the hamlet of Horton. Now follow the lane round into Horton, and go down the road, past Horton Grange.

Just after the last building on the left, leave the lane up steps at a signposted footpath. Go over a stile a few strides later and then turn right around the edge of a farm, then, with a small field in front of you, go half left across it to a step stile beside a sycamore tree, the first of a line of trees that contains ash and hawthorn. The line of trees, an adjoining raised embankment and shallow, hollow way suggest that this may have been an ancient trackway.

Follow the hedgerow to meet and cross a ditch, and then head across the ensuing field to a step stile to the right of a conspicuous gate giving access on to the A59 close to the Coronation Inn.

Cross the road with great care to a step stile near a gate on the opposite side (signposted: Stock). Over the stile the path continues at a short distance from Stock Beck, along the course of a raised embankment. The path eventually closes in on the beck, and continues over two stiles. In the next field head across, aiming slightly left, and climbing towards a wall. There is a through stile at the wall, about 150yds/m up from the beck; it is not obvious from a distance. Beyond it, keep on in the same direction, still rising, slightly left, across the slopes of Stock Hill to an unseen far corner, not far from a farm. Here you meet the Pendle Way.

Turn right on the Way, and follow a grassy path to a footbridge spanning Stock Beck. Beyond, stay with the obvious path to a stile, and then continue beside a well-established hedgerow to Bracewell Lane.

The parish church of St Michael, Bracewell, is an interesting building dating from 1153; directly opposite is the Old Post Office Cottage, which bears a plaque reading: 'These rooms were built and furnished for the residence of a schoolmaster with money arising from the sale of an organ and collections in the church Anno Domino 1867'.

At the road, turn right and go past the continuation of the Pendle Way, staying on the road for about 200yds/m, and then leaving it at a bend (signposted: Gisburn). Go across a cattle grid and follow the vehicle track. When this bears left to Calf House Laithe, branch right, keeping forward on the track, passing a pond on the edge of the Big Covert. Just after another cattle grid, leave the track, over a stile on the right and go down to cross the stream flowing into the pond, by a wooden footbridge.

Over the bridge, head across the field towards the left-hand edge of a wall, and cross the wall by a through stile. Keep on along a path into undergrowth and light woodland, following the path to a stile at the top edge, and there keeping forward across the ensuing field onto rising ground, before descending to a gate.

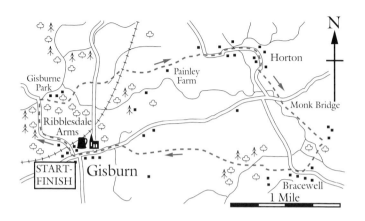

Go through the gate and down the field to three gates at the bottom. Go through the right-hand one, and then the left-hand one, heading half-right up-field towards the top edge where there is a through stile across a wall, not far from its junction with a fence. Cross the stile and go half right down the next pasture on a grassy trod to cross a stream gully and stile, and two more fields and stiles.

In the next field keep on in much the same direction, heading gently uphill towards trees on the skyline before dropping to reach another stile. Keep on beside an old hawthorn hedgerow and soon cross a narrow pasture. In the next field go forward for about 50yds/m, and then bear right, at a tree, onto a sunken trackway, then following a narrow green path that leads to a farm access. Turn right down the access to reach the A59, and there go left, with care, to return to Gisburn.

THE SPREAD EAGLE

S A W L E Y

Delightful farmland wandering, a fine viewpoint and a brief encounter with the River Ribble are all reasons for exploring Grindleton parish

DISTANCE:
6½ miles
(10km)
ALLOW:
3 hours
MAP:
OS OLM 41
TERRAIN:
Green paths across fields, quiet lanes, farm tracks and road walking.
PUBLIC TRANSPORT:
Buses to Sawley
PARKING: The Spread Eagle Hotel (ask permission first)

The original hotel building was once a part of the nearby Sawley Abbey complex, and stands by a bend in the River Ribble. The hotel bar is well-appointed and comfortable and has a friendly, welcoming atmosphere, used as much by locals as touring visitors. Walkers are welcome, as are children, but alas not dogs, though the provision of a small area with picnic tables adjoining the hotel car park means that walkers with dogs can still enjoy the hospitality of the Spread Eagle. Bar meals are served every day from 12 noon to 2.00pm and from 7.00pm to 9.00pm. Vegetarians are catered for. Tel 01200 441202.

If time allows, everyone visiting Sawley should have a look at the remains of its Cistercian abbey which was founded in 1148. It is now in the care of English Heritage, and its grounds are well tended and laid out.

Begin by walking down the Bolton-by-Bowland road, beside the River Ribble, to reach and cross Sawley Bridge. On the other side branch left

towards Grindleton and in 50yds/m turn right along a
lane leading to the Friends' Meeting House. This small
building is adjoined by a few cottages, beside which the
lane ends at a wooden gate. Go through the gate and the
next (though at the time of writing 'over' is the only way
to pass the second gate) to reach a shallow grassy runnel
rising on the left behind the Friends' Meeting House to
meet a fence.

Let the fence guide you to the top edge of a small
enclosure, gradually moving closer to a gully on the
right. Follow the gully until just before a row of cottages
you can descend to cross the gully stream by a
footbridge. Across the stream bear left and follow a field
edge past the cottages to reach a stile in a corner. Cross
this and go forward along the ensuing left-hand field
margin. When the boundary hedge bends sharply left,
keep forward to pass to the left of two trees in mid-field,

which mark the position of an old field boundary. Keep on walking in the same direction, now descending, to the bottom edge of the field. There is no path, but the stile at the bottom of the field is marked by a white disc.

Cross the stile and bear slightly right to cross a stream by a footbridge, and then keep forward in the same direction following the left-hand edge of another field, heading for a stile, marked by a white post, at the top of the field. The path rises up the edge of the next field to reach a stile in a corner. As you reach the stile there is a sign on a tree which says that the footpath to Till House Farm (which is where you are going) goes through the front garden of the house at the top of the field.

This is reassuring knowledge because this is but one of a number of places in Ribblesdale where footpaths pre-date the conversion of adjoining barns for residential purposes, and some walkers may find that walking through someone's garden, which is what invariably follows, is a disconcerting experience. No such problems arose when the buildings were used for their original farming purpose, but as planning decisions allow more of these conversions to take place it is likely that many more such situations will be met. What is important is that walkers are not discouraged from using such rights of way simply because they have been embraced by someone's private garden.

Anyway, head up the next field to another stile, and then make for the cottages and cross a stile beside a metal gate. Paved insets take the footpath across a lawn to the corner of the garden, where you can exit by a small flight of steps to gain the main access beyond. Follow the

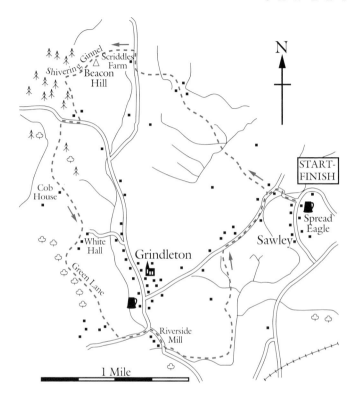

access out to cross a cattle grid and soon reach Till House Farm. The footpath goes between farm buildings to reach a quiet lane beyond.

Follow this lane until it meets a road at a T-junction. Here turn right and continue for 500yds/m, past Scriddles Farm (note the ornamental animals on the gable top), and finally leaving the road at a signposted footpath through a gate on the left, beyond which, heading directly for the white trig pillar on Beacon Hill, you follow a fence to a stile. Later you walk along the edge of raised embankments above a gully which has many hallmarks of an ancient packhorse route, and is named Shivering Ginnel. At the top cross another stile and keep forward, now with a wall on the right.

It is perfectly easy, though there is no right of way, to walk up left to the trig pillar for the fine panoramic view that this modest height affords. Pendle Hill dominates the view to the south, but in all other directions it is expansive and especially invigorating on a clear day. Return to the wall to continue.

Press on beside the wall, and through a meeting of walls, to keep forward between crumbling walls to a stile and fence, and heading towards Grindleton Forest. Much of the land to the right of the track has been cleared, but the remaining plantation lies ahead. Keep going to reach the edge of the plantation, and there cross a stile, turning immediately left as you take your leave of Shivering Ginnel, which here gallops along the lower forest edge.

Follow a pathway beside a wall and the first rank of the pines. The path wanders in and out of the trees, but generally maintains faith with the wall. At a crosspath near farm buildings, keep ahead, and soon you descend to meet a surfaced lane, with the small, distinctive rise of Simpshey Hill off to the right.

Turn right on reaching the lane and walk down it for 100yds/m to leave it at a signposted bridleway on the left, and walk forward towards a dilapidated wall, crossing the wall at a gap. This gives access to an elongated pasture, flanked by walls. Go forward into the pasture for about 80yds/m and, at the lowest point, cross the right hand wall at a gap. Stride across the next field to the gate, and then walk along a grassy path beside an on-going wall to reach another gate. Through this a delightful green lane awaits. This, sadly, is short-lived and soon becomes surfaced as Cob House Farm is reached.

Keep on down the lane until, at a junction, you are confronted with the imposing elegance of White Hall. Here turn right, following the gradually descending Green Lane until it meets the road to West Bradford, at the southern edge of the village of Grindleton. Turn left along the road, but at a bend leave it, going right on the Chatburn road for about 250yds/m to a bridge spanning the Ribble.

Do not cross the bridge, but keep to its left to gain a grassy path that follows the course of the river above embankments that in spring are colonised by families of sand martins. The path, now part of the Ribble Way, does not completely adhere to the riverbank, and is forced to leave it for a short distance at a pronounced loop in the river. A shortcut across a field, however, soon brings you back to the riverside path, and this is followed until signs direct you left to a stile giving into the edge of a field. Go forward across the field, and then the next, until you emerge on Sawley Road. Turn right along the road as far as a row of cottages overlooking the river, close by which you can return to the riverbank as far as Sawley Bridge. Leave the riverside path at the bridge, and retrace your steps to the Spread Eagle. If you begin this walk at about 9.00am, you should be back just in time for a relaxing lunch.

THE ASSHETON ARMS

D O W N H A M

*P*ush green fields, a ruined abbey and riverside strolling in the shadow of Pendle Hill

DISTANCE:
6¹/₄ miles
(10km)
ALLOW:
3 hours
MAP:
OS OLM 41
TERRAIN:
Green fields, and part of the Ribble Way. Some road walking
PUBLIC TRANSPORT:
Buses run to Downham, plus the summertime Pendle Witch Hopper
PARKING: The Assheton Arms (ask permission first). Car park in Downham

The Assheton Arms languishes in a place of age-old tranquillity, a place of architectural beauty and rural calm, where rows of stone-built cottages lead down to a duck-filled stream beneath the glowering slopes of Pendle Hill. The pub is a rambling, beamed affair that is immensely popular, and especially welcomes walkers, children and dogs. Bar meals are served every day from 12 noon to 2.00pm and from 7.00pm to 10.00pm. Vegetarians are catered for. Tel 01200 441227.

Facing the Assheton Arms go to its left along a surfaced lane in front of a cottage to a gate. Through the gate turn immediately left through another gate, and walk to a squeeze stile. Go forward beside a wall along the edge of woodland, and at a waymark keep forward, descending beside the on-going wall to reach the road into Downham at a stile.

Cross the road and go through a gate opposite, going forward down a field to another gate, to the left of

Newfield Barn Farm. From the farm descend in the same direction on a broad track at the edge of a field. The track passes beneath a railway line to a pair of gates. Go through the left gate, and keep ahead to reach a barn. Through a gap beside the barn turn immediately right walking beside a wall that borders a large pasture. When the wall bends sharply right, keep ahead to locate a gate in a field corner, beyond which you join a green path going across a low embankment to a footbridge spanning a stream. From the footbridge go forward on a green path to reach Swanside Beck where a stile through a wall gives access to an attractive single arch bridge spanning the beck.

Across the bridge and a subsequent stile, go ahead for a few strides across a level platform before ascending a little steeply, slightly left, to reach a stile across a fence. The stile brings you into a large pasture. Go across this to its far left corner on a narrow green path. In the far corner, ignore two inviting gates, but cross a fence by a stile and keep on in the same direction beside a hawthorn hedgerow. The next field, too, is accessed by a stile, beyond which the path crosses to a gate before continuing down the next field to reach the A59.

Cross this busy road with great care, and in the field beyond descend to a small ladder stile in the bottom corner. This gives on to an overgrown sunken lane, where wild garlic grows in profusion. Cross a stream, and keep on down the old lane to a gate and stile, that give access to a surfaced lane. Across the lane, tackle another stile, and go across the ensuing field to a through stile to the left of a gate. As you reach it so the remains of Sawley Abbey come into view to the left. There is no direct access to the abbey grounds from the field you are in, so descend half left across the field to meet a road near the Spread Eagle Hotel.

To visit Sawley Abbey, go left along the road, and then return to the Spread Eagle.

Sawley (Salley) Abbey was a Cistercian abbey founded in 1148. After the Dissolution of the Monasteries, which began in 1536, the monks were put back into the abbey during the Pilgrimage of Grace, and remained in possession until the uprising collapsed.

From the Spread Eagle take the road signposted to Bolton-by-Bowland, walking now with the River Ribble on your right. Keep on to cross Sawley Bridge, and then turn immediately left at a signposted path that takes you down to a riverside path, part of the Ribble Way. The path is short-lived, and returns you to the road near a row of cottages.

Turn left and follow the road for 700yds/m until you reach a footpath sign on the left as the road bends to the right. Leave the road here, and go down the ensuing field on a faint green path, aiming for the bottom end of a stream gully on the right. The path steers you to a stile in a field corner, beyond which it continues above the stream descending to another stile across a wall, with Pendle Hill occupying the whole of the skyline to the south. Over the stile turn right, and on crossing a stream, go left (Ribble Way waymark) to follow the course of the stream as it heads for the River Ribble.

The walk now follows the Ribble, targeting the steeple of Chatburn church in the distance. After following the embankment for 200yds/m a fence deflects you round to a stile. Cross this and walk across the edge of a field to another stile, that returns you to the river embankment. Now keep following the river until two stiles further on you cross a barbed wire fence to shortcut a loop in the river. A path does continue with the river, but this is not a right of way. So, leave the embankment and cut across a field, rejoining the riverbank at a stile. Turn right, and pass above embankments that in spring and summer are colonised by sand martins, and stay along the embankment until you reach a road bridge, just south of Grindleton.

Turn left over the bridge to cross the river. Walk on along the road, taking care in the absence of footpaths. After a quarter of a mile, leave the road on the left (signposted) just as it bends to the right. Ignore the broad track beyond, but branch left on a green path to return to the riverbank, and follow this to a gate, where you rejoin the

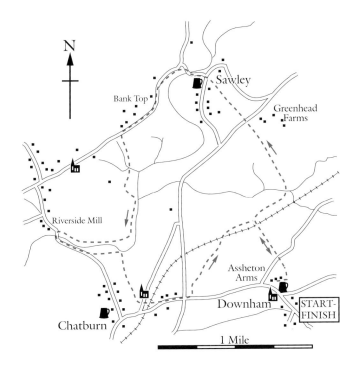

track. Beyond this, walk forward to a footbridge, after which you take your leave the of Ribble on a footpath that curves away from it to a stile.

Walk forward along a hawthorn hedgerow with the village of Chatburn just coming into view. By staying alongside the hedgerow you come to a more pronounced path, which guides you up a sloping grassy field towards the church. After a gate you go along the edge of a playing field to reach the village road near Christ Church. Cross the road and go up the lane opposite.

When the lane meets Chatburn Road turn left and cross the bridge high above the A59. Immediately turn left at a footpath sign, and follow a broad track as it descends and then bends right along a field boundary. Ignore a gate on the left and keep forward, still with the field boundary on your left and soon you reach a sunken lane that only now becomes obvious. It runs on to meet a stile beyond which it continues, flanked on both sides by hedgerows. The lane leads to a group of gates. Keep forward to cross the railway line and then turn sharp right on the continuation of the old lane, which presses on uneventfully to reach a barn encountered on the outward route. Go to the right of the barn and turn right, then retrace your steps to Downham.

THE DUKE OF YORK

G R I N D L E T O N

This visit to Bradford Fell crosses countryside populated by short-eared owls, deer, curlew, and buzzard

DISTANCE:
5¹/₂ miles (9km)
ALLOW:
2-2¹/₂ hours
TERRAIN:
Good tracks and paths, some road walking and pathless fields
MAP:
OS OLM 41
PUBLIC TRANSPORT:
Bus services operate into Grindleton from Clitheroe
PARKING: The Duke of York (ask permission first)

The Duke of York pub stands as a reminder that Grindleton was once in one of the Yorkshire Ridings. There is a patio area adjoining the pub, which is especially welcome on a warm day; at other times walkers are welcome in the bar area. Children, too, are welcome, though dogs rather less so. Bar meals, which include a small choice of dishes suitable for vegetarians, are served from Tuesday-Sunday from 12 noon to 1.45pm and from 7.00pm to 9.30pm. Tel 01200 441266.

Walk up the road beside the Duke of York, and at the Top of Town branch left on a lane that soon descends to cross Grindleton Brook before climbing to White Hall. In front of the Hall, turn right, following the lane to Cob House Farm, where the surfacing ends and you take to a delightful but brief walled green lane.

At a gate you reach the top pasture, and here go left over a rickety stile. Start down the ensuing field, following a wall. When the wall changes direction use a stile on the left to cross the continuing fence. Then go down the field on a grassy path beside the fence. At the bottom cross a footbridge.

Over the bridge bear left and follow an initially indistinct path through rushes, rising to the left-hand edge of bracken-clad Simpshey Hill ahead. The path meets a wall and here go left between walls, and onto a rising path that curves round the end of the hill, eventually running parallel with a dilapidated wall. Take care, the wall layout here is confusing. The key to success, however, is the wall on your right, below the end of Simpshey Hill. So, keep fairly close to this wall, and at a corner you discover a broad path then running almost northwards, heading for the plantation of Grindleton Forest.

This meets a rough-surfaced forest trail at a T-junction. Turn left and follow the trail, past the remains of St Clare's farmstead. When the trail next reaches a gate, near the top edge of the plantation, just after a large cleared area on the right, leave the track and go left over a stile to continue along a walled green lane. A couple of

hundred yds/m further on, at a junction, turn left onto another broad green track descending between walls. The track crosses the lower slopes of Bradford Fell.

Eventually the track runs on to meet another, Moor Lane, at a T-junction. Turn left and go through a gate, and along the lane. At the next gate keep ahead, following the lane as it bends right and left. Two gates further on you reach a barn on the left. Keep on past this, now descending with a fence on your left, as you go down beside a shallow hollow way. The track finally comes down to meet a surfaced lane, and about 80yds/m further on leave the lane, left, for a bridleway crossing a cattle grid at the entrance to Hanson's Farm.

Immediately leave the farm access, striking right to the far right-hand corner of open pasture, heading for mixed woodland. Very soon a gate comes into view. Go through it and slightly right, heading for a metal gate at the entrance to woodland flanking Drake House Brook.

Through the gate bend left and right as you descend to cross the stream at a ford. Climb out on the other side to reach the edge of the woodland at a gate. Walk the short distance across the ensuing pasture needed to pass through another gate, and then continue beside a fence towards Bucks Farm. As you approach Bucks Farm, go forward keeping the farm buildings to your left, and you'll pass in front of the farmhouse to reach its access lane. Follow this out. Immediately after a cattle grid turn left over another on a track leading to Lowcocks Farm.

Go forward into the farmyard, and on the other side go over a through stile beside a gate, and then pass to the

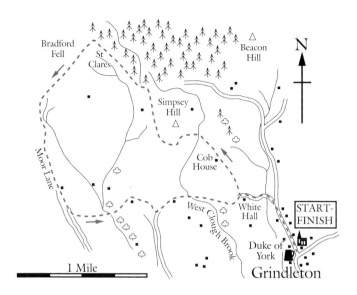

left of a water treatment works, beside which a high wall is crossed by a through stile. In the ensuing field go forward to reach woodland flanking West Clough Brook, and go down to cross the brook by a footbridge.

Keep forward to a metal gate beyond which you climb up above a hollow way, and then immediately strike right, across the field, roughly parallel with West Clough Brook, aiming for the farm buildings at White Hall. A low stile takes you on across a fence, and from it keep on in the same direction across the next two fields, crossing fences by low stiles, and across the final field heading for the left-hand edge of buildings. Leave the field at a gate and stile. Turn left, and walk the short distance to White Hall, there bearing right to retrace steps to Grindleton.

WADDINGTON ARMS

A pleasant walk across fields, quiet country lanes and a brief riparian ramble make a fine, short outing from this picturesque village

DISTANCE:
5 miles (8km)
ALLOW:
2¹/₂ hours
TERRAIN:
Easy walking;
take care on the road
MAP:
OS OLM 41
PUBLIC TRANSPORT:
Bus services run into Waddington from Clitheroe
PARKING: The Waddington Arms car park

This delightful pub enjoys a central place in the village, not far from its church, and its safe and secure beer garden is much appreciated on warm, sunny days. Walkers are especially welcome, as are children and dogs. Bar meals, which include numerous dishes and 'specials' for vegetarians, are served every day from 12 noon to 2.00pm and 7.00pm to 9.30pm. Tel 01200 423262.

Now largely inhabited by commuters and retired people, Waddington in the 19th century was bustling with farmers, tradesmen and handloom weavers, and had its own cotton spinning mill not far away. And though the centre of the village is quiet now, it was once the scene of bull-baiting and alive with the hubbub typical of the self-contained communities that flourished in this part of Yorkshire and Lancashire.

Leave the Waddington Arms and turn right to the West Bradford road. After about 100yds/m turn left on a surfaced lane (signposted:

Carter Fold Cottage). Go forward past cottages and across a cattle grid and onto a vehicle track across a field. When this bends left leave it, going forward between trees to a step stile beside a gate a short distance away.

Over the stile go towards the edge of woodland about 150yds/m away, following the remains of an old hawthorn hedge and what may be an ancient trackway. When you reach the woodland turn right beside its boundary fence and keep forward through a gate, still following the edge of the woodland which contains oak, beech, hawthorn, ash, holly and sycamore, as well as a few roe deer.

Keep following the woodland boundary until you reach a wall, and cross this on a through stile. Over the wall turn right to a farm access. Turn right along this and in a few strides go left through a metal gate, on a vehicle track to a reservoir.

Pass to the right of the reservoir compound, and then continue up-field to a step stile next to an isolated ash tree. Over the stile rejoin the edge of woodland, and keep forward along it. Stick with the woodland boundary and you will be guided down to a footbridge across a stream. Follow the on-going path around the back of a new house to a stile. Over the stile turn right and follow a path through a small estate, up a surfaced lane to a T-junction.

At the T-junction turn right, and immediately branch right at a fork to go past Cuttock Clough Farm on a rising track between farm buildings, and then keep forward over a cattle grid, and out along a rough, surfaced access lane that degenerates into a vehicle track. Continue past Seedalls Farm, and keep on in the same direction eventually swinging round to join Moor Lane, a surfaced lane. Go down the lane, passing Three Rivers Park and Country Club. When Moor Lane comes down to a T-junction in West Bradford, go left, and follow the road into the village, and take care on the road which does not have a footpath. Go past the Three Millstones pub, and take the first road on the right (signposted: Clitheroe).

Head down through the village, following the road as it reaches and then crosses the River Ribble at Bradford Bridge. Over the bridge, leave the road, on the right, on the Ribble Way. Go forward on a green path parallel with the river.

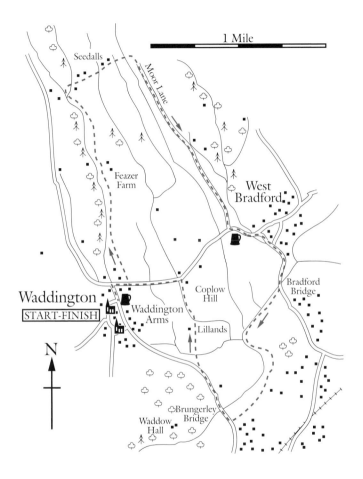

Now follow the riverside path, initially across the edge of fields, but then at a stile rising into woodland for a while. Shortly after the stile, at a path junction, turn right, and continue beside the river. The woodland forms part of the Cross Hill Quarry Local Nature Reserve, and is popular locally.

Always stay with the path that parallels the river, and shortly pass an interesting mile post. Keep on with the Ribble Way to meet the B6478 near Brungerley Bridge. At the road turn right and cross the bridge, on which there is a reminder that Waddington was once in Yorkshire, and that the river then formed the boundary between Lancashire and Yorkshire – it's all Lancashire now.

Before the bridge was built in 1816, the river was crossed here at peril on a line of stepping stones, the Brungerley Hippings. These became more difficult to cross in the 18th century following the construction of a weir just below Waddow Hall, which caused the river to deepen and widen.

Go past the driveway to Waddow Hall and 100yds/m further on, leave the road, on the right, through a kissing gate at a signposted footpath. Go down a surfaced access track that crosses Waddington Brook to Lillands Farm. Pass Lillands to a gate, and beyond the gate take to a grassy track. Go forward, to the left of a barn, and then keep along the line of a fence below the low mound of Coplow Hill. Cross a stile and go forward to a fence gap, and then across to the top right-hand corner of the next field, where a stile gives access to the Waddington-West Bradford road.

Turn left along the road and walk back into Waddington. A footpath on the right, shielded from traffic by a hedgerow, provides safe walking.

THE BAYLEY ARMS

A fine old college and two rivers await the visitor to this charming corner of Lancashire

DISTANCE:
5½ miles (9km)
ALLOW:
2½ hours
TERRAIN:
Field, farm and riverside paths
MAP: OS Pathfinder 680
PUBLIC TRANSPORT:
The Clitheroe-Longridge bus service passes through Hurst Green
PARKING:
Bayley Arms car park (ask permission first)

The Bayley Arms is a very popular pub, and evidences its support for walkers by producing its own walks booklet detailing four walks around the area. Children, too, are welcome, as are well-behaved dogs. Bar meals are served every day from 12 noon to 2.00pm and 7.00pm to 9.30pm, and include a selection of dishes for vegetarians. Tel 01254 826478.

It may come as a surprise to learn that Hurst Green has been a popular 'tourist' destination for many years. Horse-drawn carriages or waggonettes, and later charabancs, brought visitors to the village, and cyclists, myself included, would often add the village to their day's itinerary. Quite a few of the cottages provided teas, and there used to be two ferries to carry people across the river.

From the Bayley Arms turn right and walk up the road past Shireburn House, turning right into Smithy Row.

Keep on past the last of a row of

cottages, on a path to a kissing gate, beyond which go forward along a left-hand field edge. A couple of fields further on, follow the boundary of Fox Fall Wood, and then gradually move across an elongated pasture to follow an iron fence on the right to a gate at the top of the field. Go through the gate, which gives access into the grounds of Stonyhurst College.

Stonyhurst College, which is open to the public, is a magnificent 16th-century manor house that became home to a Catholic independent boarding school. The Hall was begun in 1590 by Sir Richard Shireburn and occupied as the family seat until 1794, when the estate was given to the Society of Jesus.

Turn right past the observatory to Hall Barns Farm. Do not enter the farmyard, but turn left just on reaching it onto a grassy path beside buildings, and head towards an ivy-covered cottage. Go past the cottage and beside a tall brick wall to reach a surfaced track. At a cross-track a few strides further on go forward and follow the on-going track until it meets a road. Cross the road obliquely left, and then go down another surfaced lane between cottages, keeping forward onto a rough track.

As you approach woodland leave the track, branching right at a white waymark sign to enter a large open pasture. Go forward, keeping with a hedgerow on your left, until, at a stile, you can enter the edge of the woodland and follow a narrow path, with a steep, wooded drop on the left, before going down steps into the woodland to cross a stream by a footbridge. Having done so, ignore ascending paths on the left, and keep forward, still descending, and then recross the stream at an old, single arch bridge. Climb a stony path back into woodland, with the River Hodder audible on your left, and then descend, below the walls of Hodder Place, to cross the edge of farmland and reach a footpath beside the river. The path runs on, beside the river, to reach the road at Lower Hodder Bridge.

Nearby are the remains of an old bridge by means of which Cromwell is said to have crossed the river as he passed this way to engage the Royalists at Preston. The bridge predates this time, but is known locally as Cromwell Bridge. A brief detour on to Lower Hodder Bridge will bring it into view.

At the road, turn right and walk for about a quarter of a mile to a road junction, then leaving the road, on the left, over a ladder stile, at a signposted footpath. Go into the field, to a stile at a hedge gap, having now joined the Ribble Way. Go up the left edge of the next field to another stile, and then continue above the edge of Spring Wood, until you can bear right across a field to an iron kissing gate.

Go across the ensuing field to a gate on the opposite side, and then turn left on a surfaced lane, and go past the entrance to Winckley Hall, where the surfacing ends and a rough track takes over, descending to Winckley Hall Farm. Go forward into the farmyard, and follow a waymarked route between buildings to reach a broad track not far from the Hodder. Turn right along this, and keep forward through a metal gate and on along the on-going track, now directly opposite the confluence between the Hodder and the Ribble.

As the river makes a wide loop the riverside path branches away towards a derelict cottage – Hacking Boat House, a reminder of the days when a ferry operated here, between Hacking and Winckley – and then continues along a field margin a short distance from the river. It goes on to reach Jumbles Farm, near Jumbles Rocks, a small rock step that brings the river to life.

Go past the farm, on an access track, and when this bends right towards Fox Fields Farm, leave it, on the left, returning to a riverside path. Keep on past an aqueduct, from where a path runs on to a stile at the field edge, beyond which a footbridge crosses a stream. Steps now take you up into woodland.

At the top edge of the woodland, cross another stile, then go forward on a green path with the woodland edge on your right, and soon descending into woodland to cross a couple of stiles in quick succession, and then going forward on a path across an undulating pasture, continuing up-field between two shallow gullies, each intermittently lined with trees. Part way up the field you meet a rough track. Turn right on this, then bearing left

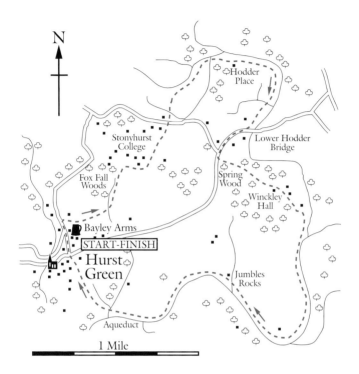

to go up towards the village. Keep near the left-hand field edge, which brings you to a couple of gates. Go over a through stile between the gates, and then up to reach the car park of the Shireburn Arms. Past this you reach the village road. Go across, and up the lane opposite to return to the Bayley Arms.

THE WHITE BULL

RIBCHESTER

℞ oman antiquity, riverside walking and bright green fields are a lure anywhere, but around Ribchester they have special appeal

DISTANCE:
4 miles (6.5km)
ALLOW:
2-2¹/₂ hours
MAP: OS
Pathfinder 680
TERRAIN:
Farm tracks,
green fields and
quiet lanes
PUBLIC
TRANSPORT:
Buses run to
Ribchester
PARKING:
There is a large
public car park
in the centre of
Ribchester

The White Bull is an 18th-century inn (dated 1707), and the four columns supporting the entrance porch are thought to be of Roman origin, having been dredged from the River Ribble. There is a walled garden for children to play in, and walkers are very welcome, but no dogs, please. Vegetarians are catered for, and the chef is willing to meet any such special requirements, if possible. Bar meals are served Sunday 12 noon to 8.00pm; Monday to Saturday 11.30am to 2.00pm and 6.30pm to 9.30pm (except Mondays). Tel 01254 878303.

Ribchester is built on the site of a Roman-British settlement, and is the only village that stands on the banks of the River Ribble. The village, once renowned for handloom weaving, is surrounded by attractive farmland, and in Roman times was called Bremetennacum Veteranorum.

From the car park walk up into the centre of the village (signposted to the Roman Museum), and turn right into Church Street to pass the White Bull. Keep following the road round to the right, with the river on your left. The Roman Museum lies a short way down the road, and is well worth a visit.

The museum stands on the site of the main building of the Roman fort which was established in AD78 under the governorship of Julius Agricola. The original fort was of turf and timber, and was rebuilt in stone about AD100 and then occupied for some 300 years. The fort accommodated 500 cavalry, which included soldiers from Spain (Asturians) and, later, Hungary (Sarmatians).

The nearby church of St Wilfrid is a delightful construction, and was built in the 13th century on the site of a pre-Norman church.

Keep on following the road to Lower Alston Farm, passing through the farmyard, and leaving it on a surfaced track between hawthorn hedgerows to Lower Barn Farm. Keep on past Lower Barn and then Boat House Farm, with the Ribble on the left getting ever closer. After a stile you are directly above the river, following a fenceline to a gate.

Beyond the gate go forward, ascending through trees along the upper edge of a small woodland to cross a small hillock, before descending to a farm access track. Turn left down the track and press on to Hothersall Hall Farm, and there climb away from it on a concrete access lane. At the top of a rise about 80yds/m further on, leave the lane, branching right through a gate and walking upfield to another gate a short distance ahead. In the ensuing field follow the track around the field edge, and keep on to a gate at a field corner (fence and hedgerow). Go forward through the gate and keep on in the same direction across the pasture beyond to a high fence and gate.

Through the gate go along a broad grassy track between fences, and when this ends at a surfaced farm access keep forward. At a T-junction adjoining Ox Hey Farm, turn left for 30yds/m, and then go right, through a gate and along the double tracks of a bridleway. This leads into a large open pasture. Go forward across it and within a few strides you can see ahead the gate you should be aiming for. Through the gate keep left along the top of a stream gully until the path drops into a dip to a gate. Rise beyond into a field, where the path becomes indistinct. Keep going forward to pass just to the right of a small copse containing a pond, and then bear half right across the field to the far corner aiming for a white gatepost.

A short length of track leads to another gate and a large open field. Go diagonally left across the field, targeting a

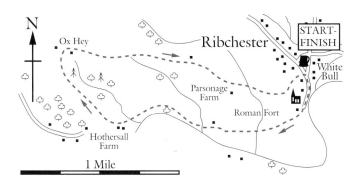

tall chimney you can now see ahead. This line brings you to the edge of another pasture (gate) in which you descend with the right-hand hedgerow to Parsonage Farm. As you approach the farm you are funnelled down between two hedgerows and through two gates to reach a surfaced lane.

Turn left and in a few strides follow the lane, right, descending to cross fields. The lane leads directly back to the car park in Ribchester.

THE DOG INN

*F*ounded on its Cistercian abbey and even older church, Whalley is an excellent launch pad from which to spring out onto the expanse of Wiswell Moor

DISTANCE:
5 miles (8km)
ALLOW:
2¹/₂ hours
TERRAIN:
Generally good paths and tracks
MAP: OS Pathfinder 680
PUBLIC TRANSPORT:
Many bus services operate to Whalley
PARKING: The Dog Inn does not have a car park, but there are a number of car parks nearby

The Dog Inn stands in the centre of Whalley, not far from the abbey, and happily caters for walkers, being particularly proud of its warm welcome and home-cooked food. Children and dogs are welcome, and bar meals, which include choices for vegetarians, are served every day from 12 noon to 2.00pm, except Christmas Day and New Year's Day. Tel 01254 823009.

Leave Whalley along the main road heading towards Clitheroe. Go past the Methodist church until, at Forge Corner, you can turn right on a footpath into Brookes Lane, and at the end of the lane bear right, past a farm, following a broad surfaced track beside a stream. When you next reach a gate, branch right, down to cross a stream. Turn left to go up a field with the stream on your left. When you reach a small woodland, cross a stile to enter it, following a clear path over a footbridge and continuing to pass beneath the A671, beyond which you enter Spring

Wood. As you do, bear right and keep going until you reach a car park.

Walk out from the car park to the main road and turn left for a short distance until you can go through a gap in a wall and onto a golf course. Keep well to the left and follow the edge of the golf course and Spring Wood until at the top end of the wood, which in spring is full of bluebells and wild garlic, you reach a footbridge spanning a small stream. Cross this and go ahead across the ensuing field to reach a fence. Follow the fence up-field to a stile. Cross this stile and walk on a short distance to another stile. Cross this, too, and the one that immediately follows.

Now go left along a fenceline to reach a broad track. Nearby you will find a bench bequeathed for the use of walkers in this area by the late Jessica Lofthouse, a much-respected observer of all country matters throughout her native North West. You'll encounter more of these benches during this walk.

Turn left on the track and follow it to the edge of Deer Park Wood. Go into the wood and keep forward along the path ahead which leads to a ladder stile. Beyond the stile, keep forward, slightly left, on a descending green path across an open pasture to a series of gates to reach a lane. Turn left, descending to reach the village of Wiswell.

As you reach Wiswell, cross the road, and go ahead to pass the Freemason's Arms to another T-junction. Turn left and immediately right on a signposted footpath adjoining Arnside House. This leads to a stile next to a greenhouse. Cross this and follow the path beyond through shrubbery adjoining a fence to reach an open pasture at a stile.

Go down the field to a gate and stile. Having crossed this stile turn sharp right to another. Cross that, too, and turn left to go down-field, following a fence and hedgerow. At the bottom of the field you meet the A59, a busy and frantic dual carriageway that needs to be crossed with care.

Ascend a pathway on the other side, rising to a field. Ignore a stile on the right, and go forward down the field with a well-established hedgerow on your right. More stiles guide you down the field to a large open lawned area adjoining a house. As you reach this, go slightly right into shrubbery in a corner, to a stile. Cross this and go forward to reach Whalley Road at a stile.

Cross Whalley Road, and a stile on the other side to gain

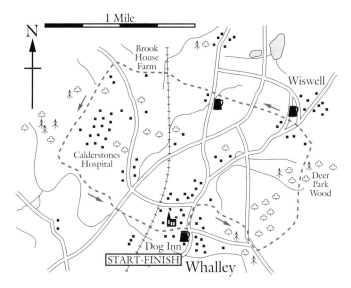

access to a very large open pasture, and keep forward down the field, descending gently beside a hedgerow and ditch. The path brings you down to the railway line. Cross this with care, and the stile on the other side, continuing on a pathway below a slightly raised embankment and between trees to cross a stream by a footbridge, and going forward into the field beyond.

Then follow a fence and hedgerow to another footbridge beyond which you reach a broad track. Turn left along this to reach Brook House Farm. Go past most of the farm buildings, but turn right along a track through a gate that takes you into a very large field, sometimes used for caravan rallies. Keep forward into the large field, but look for a gap in a hedgerow on the left. Having gone through the gap, turn right and follow the hedge for some distance until you can bear left to a stile adjoining the Great Mitton road. Cross the road, and go forward on a broad track that leads on for some distance to pass Calderstones Hospital.

When the track reaches two gates, go over the stile to the left of the left-hand gate, and follow perimeter fencing to a gate, keeping on along the track beyond, with the River Calder appearing on the right. About 200yds/m after the gate, leave the track, bearing right along a hawthorn hedgerow above the river. A path runs beside this, to go down to the river. Turn left up-river for 200yds/m until you encounter a fence on the edge of the sewage works. Turn left along this, and keep on along the perimeter fence to reach a rough track that leads you on to rejoin the River Calder, and forward beneath the A59 and on to the massive Whalley viaduct. Go under the viaduct and past the gatehouse to Whalley Abbey, following the road into the centre of the town.

While in Whalley it is well worth visiting the Abbey, an impressive complex of buildings, still in use for conferences and so on, and managed by the Blackburn Diocese.

THE CRAWFORD ARMS

*T*he various attractions of Haigh Country Park, former home of the Earls of Crawford, are visited on this easy walk

DISTANCE:
3¹/₂ miles (6km)
ALLOW:
1¹/₂ hours
TERRAIN:
Footpaths, towpath and lanes
MAPS: OS Pathfinders 711 and 712
PUBLIC TRANSPORT:
Buses operate from Wigan to Red Rock
PARKING:
Crawford Arms (but ask permission first)

Sitting beside the Leeds and Liverpool Canal, the Crawford Arms is a popular pub throughout the year and provides a good range of meals and drinks. Walkers are always welcome, as are children, though dogs are restricted to an outside patio. Bar meals and snacks, which include a selection for vegetarians, are served on Mondays 12 noon to 2.00pm; Tuesday-Saturday 12 noon to 2.00pm and 5.30pm to 9.00pm; Sundays 12 noon to 8.00pm. Tel 01257 421313.

The walk begins along the towpath, heading south towards the distant woodland of Haigh Country Park. Easy walking along the towpath ensues, flanked by farm fields and, beyond Sennicar Lane, by the fairways of Haigh Golf Course.

The Leeds and Liverpool Canal was one of three canals built in response to the need to link the industrial towns of South Yorkshire with Manchester and Liverpool. It was the third such to be built – the others were the Rochdale Canal and the

Huddersfield Narrow Canal – and was constructed between 1770 and 1816 The canal is 127 miles long with 91 locks (142 miles and 104 locks if you include branches), and commercial traffic was still using the canal until the 1960s.

The main drive through Haigh Country Park, and up to the impressive Hall, crosses the canal by an iron trellis bridge. Leave the towpath on the right, when you reach it, and ascend to the driveway. Turn left and across the canal, and a short way on branch left to follow a rough track through woodland that takes you off the surfaced drive for a while.

When the main drive is encountered again, cross it, and go ahead on a rough track. Soon, you cross the miniature railway that operates during summer months. Keep on in the same direction, passing a pond, known to the Crawfords as the Swan Pond, and eventually the track

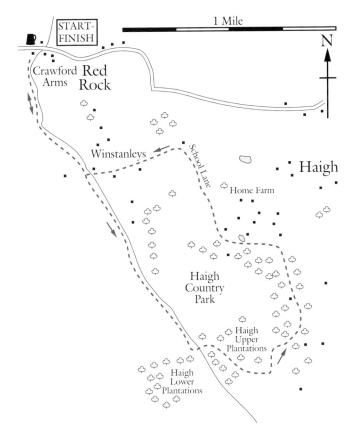

brings you to a children's play area adjoining the stables block, which houses a cafe and information centre/gift shop. Haigh Hall is off to your left, and to reach it you need to branch left as you reach the children's play area.

In the 12th century the manor of Haigh was held by a Norman, Hugh le Norreys, and by 1295 it was the property of Mabel, who was married to Sir William Bradshaigh. The Hall is the second to be built on this site, being constructed during the reign of George IV by James, who became the 24th Earl of Crawford in 1825 and was made Baron Wigan of Haigh Hall. Work began on the Hall in 1827 and was finished around 1840 (some sources say 1849). The old hall had been significantly enlarged during the reign of Elizabeth I, but was later much neglected. It was to Earl James that the task of rebuilding fell. Fortunately, he was an engineer, and drew his own plans, directed the building operations himself, and used his own materials.

His successor, the 25th Earl of Crawford, who was an accomplished scholar and traveller, amassed a library of great value, much of which was transferred to the John Rylands Library in Manchester. The library contained more than 5,000 manuscripts dating from the sixth century, many written on tree bark, papyrus and vellum.

Having visited the Hall (not open to the public), go round the building and continue ahead, passing the stables, to reach and cross the main car park. As you leave the car park, turn left on a narrow lane, taking great care against approaching traffic since there is no footpath here. Continue as far as the second turning on your left, Pendlebury Lane, and go down this to rejoin the canal.

Just over the canal bridge you can descend left (slippery when wet) to reach the towpath. Go under the bridge and follow the towpath pleasantly back to the Crawford Arms.

THE ORWELL

A** taste of nostalgia and the easiest of walking awaits visitors to **Wigan Pier

DISTANCE:
4¹/₂ miles (7km)
(in each
direction)
ALLOW:
2 hours (each
way)
TERRAIN:
Easy towpath
walking
MAP: OS
Pathfinder 711
PUBLIC
TRANSPORT:
Many bus and
rail services run
into Wigan, and
trains run back
from Appley
Bridge at 24
minutes past
each hour (but
check the times
before leaving)
PARKING: The
Orwell at Wigan
Pier

The Orwell, adjoining the Leeds and Liverpool Canal, forms part of the Wigan Pier complex, a popular tourist attraction. Time should be allowed to visit 'The Way We Were' exhibition and the mill engine at Trencherfield Mill. Walkers are welcome, as are children, but dogs will need to be left outside. Bar meals, which include at least three choices every day suitable for vegetarians, are served from 12 noon to 2.30pm on Mondays to Saturdays, and on Sundays from 12.30pm to 3.00pm. Tel 01942 323034.

The walk is very straightforward, being linear. You can either retrace your steps from Appley Bridge, no less a pleasant experience for reversing the outward process, or catch a train back into Wigan. The canal is an interesting companion for the entire walk, and for much of the way so is the River Douglas, which is born far away on the boggy slopes of Winter Hill. Quite a range of birds frequents both the canal and the Douglas, the latter at times coming quite close to the canal.

I used to run this route every day during my lunch break when I worked in Wigan and needed to escape the machinations of the office for a while. During the fishing season the canal banks were often populated by anglers with roach poles that reached from the back of the towpath well out into the canal; not many will have done the nine-mile hurdles on a daily basis!

From the Orwell go past the souvenir shop and across the footbridge towards the road bridge carrying Wallgate out of town; this is a changeline bridge, a reminder of the days when barges were pulled by horses. This type of bridge was the method adopted to accomplish the task of getting horses and barges back into the correct relationship at complex junctions or direction changes before resuming the onward journey.

Cross the pedestrian bridge and go onto the canal side,

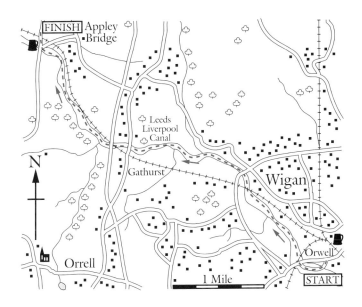

soon reaching a pair of metal stanchions at the canal edge, directly opposite the Wigan Pier Centre. This metal construction was the means by which wagons of coal, etc., were emptied into the canal barges, and the centre has a display explaining how this all worked.

Now all that remains is to walk beside the canal for as long as you want. It is never unpleasant, and provides the easiest of walking. One suitable place at which to take a break is the Navigation Inn at Gathurst, but if you want to press on further to take the train back, the towpath keeps on beneath the M6 and on to Appley Bridge, where finally you leave it for the village, or turn round and head back to Wigan.

EAGLE AND CHILD

O ften well-populated in winter by wildfowl, the farmlands south-east of Rufford offer easy walking, and a chance to visit Rufford Hall

DISTANCE:
6 miles (10km)
ALLOW:
3 hours
TERRAIN:
Farm tracks and country lanes
MAP: OS Pathfinder 699
PUBLIC TRANSPORT:
Bus services operate to Bispham Green, and a rail service to Rufford
PARKING: The Eagle and Child

The Eagle and Child is a popular pub, with a reputation that reaches far beyond the surrounding villages. Walkers are always welcome here, as are children, but dogs will need to be left outside. Bar meals, which include selections for vegetarians, are served Monday to Saturday from 12 noon to 2.00pm and 6.00pm to 8.30pm; Sundays 12 noon to 8.30pm. Tel 01257 462297.

From the Eagle and Child turn right, along Maltkiln Lane and go up past Crookell's Farm to a T-junction with School Lane. Continue left along School Lane and into Daub Lane to reach a farm shop. Turn right, and then left at a footpath sign. Keep close to the on-going field boundary, to cross the River Douglas by a footbridge, and then go round a barn to a stile.

Waymarks now guide you across the open fields that lie ahead. If you have a dog, please keep it on a lead, since the fields here are often grazed by sheep, especially during winter.

Eventually, the walk runs out to meet another lane. Turn right and keep on as far as the Leeds-Liverpool Canal, and there leave the lane to go right, along the towpath, following this to Rufford. The walk continues to the right, and over White Bridge, when Rufford is reached, but anyone wanting to visit Rufford Hall should go left to the A59, and then right, to reach the entrance.

Rufford Old Hall, a National Trust property, is one of the finest buildings in Lancashire, possessing a Tudor Hall, timber framed in late medieval style. It was the home of the Hesketh family for 400 years. By the middle of the 18th century, manor houses were considered unsuited to domestic life, and the family vacated the hall around 1760 and moved to Rufford New Hall, though the Old Hall was reoccupied from around 1825 until 1936.

The walk resumes from the Leeds and Liverpool Canal, along the village lane. Follow it to White Bridge, where it crosses the River Douglas, and go round the bend ahead. Stay along the road for about 150yds/m to a footpath sign on the left. Go left, and alongside a ditch to the far corner of the field. Go right, over a grassy bridge, to reach a farm access. Follow this for half a mile or so to reach New Reed Brook. Leave the access track here and walk along the top of the bank, past a farm bridge, to reach another track.

Turn right for 100yds/m, then right again over a sleeper bridge, then immediately left, following the field margin to Black Moor Road. Turn right as far as Sandy Lane, and then left, shortly turning left again to pursue a many-stiled route, past an equestrian centre, and ahead across a lane, continuing then to reach School Lane.

Go along School Lane to reach Maltkiln Lane, and then go left to return to the Eagle and Child.

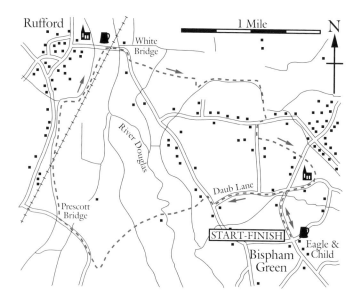

STRAWBURY DUCK

*T*his walk around the Jumbles and Wayoh Reservoirs also visits Turton Tower, set amid beautiful grounds

DISTANCE:
6 miles (10km)
ALLOW:
3-4 hours
TERRAIN:
Easy walking on
good paths
MAP:
OS Explorer 19
PUBLIC
TRANSPORT:
A number of
bus companies
operate along
Bradshaw Road,
and a rail service
stops close by at
Entwistle station
PARKING: The
Strawbury Duck
(but ask
permission first)

The Strawbury Duck is a popular pub, and rightly so. It is a Mecca for walkers who visit the nearby reservoirs and moors, and children are welcome, too, though dogs cannot be allowed into the pub. Bar meals, which include a selection of dishes for vegetarians, are served on Mondays from 7.00pm to 10.00pm; Tuesday to Friday from 12 noon to 2.00pm and 7.00pm to 10.00pm; Saturday 12 noon to 10.00pm and Sundays 12 noon to 9.30pm. Tel 01204 852013.

From the pub cross the nearby railway line, and at a low stile on the left a short way on, cross into a field and follow a path through woodland to two wooden bridges at the top end of Wayoh Reservoir. Now continue through woodland down the eastern side of the reservoir. This is an important area for birdwatching, and nearly 150 species have been recorded here.

When you reach Hob Lane, which crosses the reservoir, keep forward on a path along the eastern edge of

the reservoir, as it continues and climbs to a fine vantage point near the south-eastern corner. The path descends to the reservoir at the corner of the Wayoh embankment, and from there leave the reservoir to press on in the same direction to the road at the southern end of Edgworth.

Walk down the road to Turton Bottoms. Cross Bradshaw Brook on the road bridge, and about 100yds/m further on go left on a path that goes back down to recross the brook. Now follow Bradshaw Brook southwards. The valley gradually opens out as you approach Jumbles Reservoir before continuing down the eastern side to the Waterfold Car Park Information Centre.

Turn left and walk through the main car park following the footpath down the embankment at the southern end of the reservoir, and descend steps to a stile at the end of a bridge. Take the path on the left, towards Ousel Nest

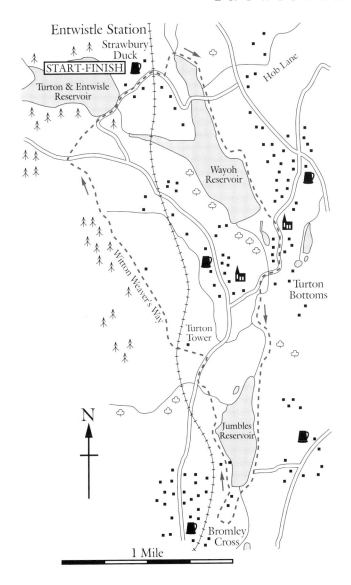

Entwistle Station

Strawbury Duck

START-FINISH

Turton & Entwistle Reservoir

Hob Lane

Wayoh Reservoir

Witton Weaver's Way

Turton Bottoms

Turton Tower

N

Jumbles Reservoir

Bromley Cross

1 Mile

Field Cottage, and follow a hedgerow to the right until the path meets Grange Road at another stile. Turn right.

Continue along Grange Road, and past Ousel Nest car park, to pass through the gates of Grange Farm, walking along an avenue of trees. At the farm go through the stables and on to the reservoir path, and continue past sailing club buildings, and up Horrobin Lane. At the top of Horrobin Lane turn right and cross Chapeltown Road (B6391), taking care on this busy road. Follow the road, uphill, to the turning to Turton Tower, on the left.

Turton Tower was originally a pele tower, probably 15th-century. It was refashioned and extended in the 16th century by William Orrell, though much of the ornate timbering is the work of Joseph (or James) Kay, a cotton spinner from Preston, who bought the estate in 1835.

Go past the tower and soon you will cross over the Blackburn to Bolton railway line, then bearing right beside a stream as the route sweeps out onto rough moorland. Now follow a clear path past Clough House Farm, to meet Greens Arms Road (B6391). At the road turn right for about 80yds/m, and then branch left, following a path down to the Batridge car park, near the dam of the Turton and Entwistle Reservoir.

Off to your right you can see Wayoh Reservoir once more, which opened in 1876 as a compensation reservoir, supplying water for industry in the Bradshaw valley.

From the car park walk to the far side of Turton and Entwistle embankment, continuing ahead along Overshores Road to reach the Strawbury Duck.

ROYAL OAK HOTEL

his walk circles around Hoghton Tower, the ancestral home of the de Hoghton family

DISTANCE:
3 miles (5km)
ALLOW:
2 hours
TERRAIN:
Easy lanes, tracks, and field paths, and woodland
MAP: OS Pathfinder 689
PUBLIC TRANSPORT:
Stagecoach Ribble operate services between Preston and Blackburn that pass through Hoghton and Riley Green
PARKING: The Royal Oak (but ask permission first)

Riley Green lies to the south of the knoll on which Hoghton Tower, a familiar Lancashire landmark, was built. The hotel here, which has been a pub since the early 18th century, welcomes walkers. Children and dogs are welcome, too, in certain rooms. Bar meals, which usually include a choice of four main courses for vegetarians, are served from 12 noon to 2.00pm and 6.00pm to 9.00pm, every day. Tel 01254 201445.

Beside the Royal Oak turn immediately right along what used to be the driveway to Hoghton Tower. Keep on until you pass Green Lane Farm, and here branch left, striking across fields and through more trees to reach the present driveway to the hall.

If you are doing this walk on a Sunday, or on a Saturday during July and August, Hoghton Tower is open to the public, and well worth a visit. The Tower, built during the time of Elizabeth I, stands on the site of the ancestral home of the de Hoghton family since the early part of the 14th century, and is still in the de Hoghton family ownership. King James I was entertained here in 1617, during the course of which the king is said to have knighted an especially succulent loin of beef, which thereafter became known as sirloin.

Go forward across the driveway, bearing right around a field margin until you reach a fence. Cross a stile and turn left to reach Chapel Lane. Turn right and follow the lane until, after about half a mile it crosses a bridge. Go down the track on the right immediately after the bridge, which progressively descends through sparse woodland and past ruined buildings to reach the River Darwen. As you reach the river go right, along its footpath, and soon pass beneath the railway viaduct with the steep rocky cone on which Hoghton Tower stands towering above.

Woodland also accompanies the river and is particularly attractive in spring and early summer when the many birds that shelter there are busy with their offspring.

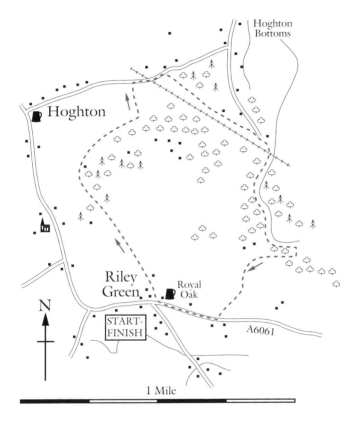

Cross a footbridge and continue to a stile at the edge of the wood, with a level riverside meadow flowing on ahead. Here turn right, uphill on a stony track back through woodland and out into open fields. The on-going track, past a cottage, then runs on to reach the A6061 a short distance east of Riley Green. Turn right along the A6061 to return to the Royal Oak.

THE ANCHOR INN

C urious heads, canals and stretches of the Pendle Way find a place in this walk to the south of Barnoldswick

DISTANCE:
5¹/₂ miles (9km)
ALLOW:
2¹/₂ hours
TERRAIN:
Canalside paths, lanes and farm tracks
MAP:
OS OLM 41
PUBLIC TRANSPORT:
Buses run to Salterforth from Barnoldswick and Colne
PARKING: The Anchor Inn (ask permission first)

In such a prime position beside the Leeds and Liverpool Canal, the Anchor Inn is popular with canal holiday-makers and locals. The inn welcomes walkers and children (there is an outdoor play area), and dogs are welcome in the garden, and in the pub outside catering hours. Bar meals, including a small selection for vegetarians, are served between 12 noon and 2.00pm and 7.00pm to 9.00pm. Tel 01282 813186.

At the Anchor Inn gain the towpath of the Leeds and Liverpool Canal and go under Bridge 151, and follow the towpath. Keep on under the main roadbridge a short way on, and go as far as Cockshott Bridge, which immediately precedes Lower Park Marina. Cross the bridge and go up the field beyond on a broad grassy trail to a surfaced lane. Turn left and walk up to the main road.

At the road turn left and cross it (with care), and 80yds/m further on (and no more) turn right, up a rising track beside a large house to reach an open field. Follow a vehicle track rising along the left edge of the field to a gate at a hedgerow corner. Through the gate go slightly right across the ensuing field to a gap stile. Go through the stile and forward to a car parking area that forms part of a small recreation area. Keep forward across the car park and leave the recreation area on a surfaced lane that descends to meet the B6251 at a T-junction.

Turn right and immediately left onto a lane going down past cottages towards Moor Side Farm. Past the cottages the lane becomes walled on both sides as it climbs easily towards the farm. About 100yds/m before the farm turn right through a gate and go forward alongside a wall (ignore a gap on the left), and cross it at a through stile (not instantly obvious) about half-way along the wall, then continue beside the wall again to a gap stile at a wall corner.

Beyond the stile, go forward with a fenceline on your right. Keep on in the same direction to meet a stream. Cross a stile and turn right beside a wall, with the stream on your left, and keep on to a narrow footbridge. Cross this and then go half left up the field beyond to a corner, and there go through an old gateway until just past a building you need to look for a low step stile and wall gap stile on the right by means of which you can reach the field in front of the building and across to its access lane. Follow this part-surfaced vehicle track out to meet Folly Lane at a T-junction.

Turn left and ascend Folly Lane and keep going past Craven View Farm and Higher View Farm, where the surfaced lane ends to become an on-going grassy track between walls. When the track ends at a gate and stile, go forward between a wall and an old hawthorn hedgerow towards Duck Pond Farm. As you reach the farm, go left and then right, passing in front of the farm buildings to a gate. Note the intriguing sculptures here.

Beyond Duck Pond Farm follow a grassy path across the ensuing field to a gate in the distance, where Blacko Tower, a folly, comes into view. From the gate keep forward across heather moorland, on a narrow trod, descending to a gate in a wall corner. Go left through the gate, and 70yds/m further on turn right at another gate to follow a vehicle track beside a wall down to meet Gisburn Old Road.

Turn left for 70yds/m and then leave it on the right at a small gated wall gap giving access to an elongated pasture. Cross this to the wall opposite and keep on across a couple of stiles to a through stile on the right.

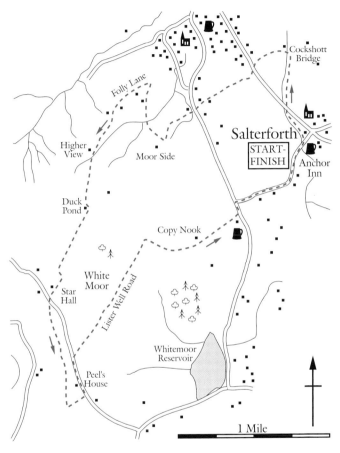

Over the stile turn left to a step stile beside a gate
(20yds/m) onto a walled lane. The lane leads back to
Gisburn Old Road. Turn left and walk past Peel's House,
and 80yds/m further on leave the road, on the right,
through a gate. Go forward beside a wall, and at a gate
the path joins Lister Well Road, a broad walled lane,

probably an old drove road or salt track. Keep following the lane to a footpath sign on the right, from where there is a sudden and splendid view northwards over the Yorkshire Dales, with Ingleborough and Penyghent conspicuous in the far distance.

Leave the walled lane, over a through stile beside a gate, and follow the on-going vehicle track across heather moorland. Cross an intermediate wall at a gate, and go down the ensuing field to a gate and stile at the bottom. This gives on to a walled lane that goes down past Copy Nook Farm, to meet the B6251 at the Fanny Grey pub.

Turn left and cross the road, and after 100yds/m turn right on the road descending for a speedy return to the Anchor Inn at Salterforth.

THE MOORCOCK INN

𝓕 ine moorland views and canalside walking are a feature of this lovely walk in East Lancashire

DISTANCE:
5¹/₂ miles (9km)
ALLOW:
2¹/₂ hours
TERRAIN:
Easy; mostly on good paths
MAP:
OS OLM 41
PUBLIC TRANSPORT:
Buses operate along the road past the Moorcock Inn
PARKING:
Moorcock Inn (but ask permission first)

In a superb position high on the moors, this isolated old inn has outstanding views from the big picture windows in its spacious bar, which has a lofty ceiling and walls hung with brass ornaments. Walkers are welcome, as are children and dogs, and an imaginative selection of meals includes dishes for vegetarians. Bar meals are served every day from 12 noon to 2.00pm and from 6.00pm to 9.30pm. Tel 01282 614186.

Leave the Moorcock Inn and turn left down the road taking care as you do so along this busy road. As you go down the road Stansfield Tower comes into view ahead on a low, domed hill.

The tower is a small, castellated folly built in 1891 by Jonathan Stansfield as a look-out, in the hope he might catch sight of his girlfriend who lived in Gisburn, four miles to the north.

After 300yds/m leave the road at a through stile near a gate, where the Pendle Way is joined. Beyond the stile descend left on a grassy path,

and soon, on reaching a shallow gully, descend right, to a stream in the bottom of the valley.

The stream is crossed by a huge single slab of stone that may be an ancient 'clam' bridge. Cross the nearby stile and go forward on a grassy path parallel with Admergill Water. The path moves away from the stream slightly, and leads to another stile, then continuing as a grassy track beside a wall. At a stile beside a gate you reach a surfaced lane. Go forward along this to pass Admergill Hall, and keep on over a cattle grid. Turn right at a Pendle Way waymark descending to cross Admergill Water again, near Admergill Barn, now a house. Go through a gate and across the gravelled forecourt of the house to two gates at the far side. Through a kissing gate strike across the ensuing field to a footpath sign at a bridge. Cross the bridge to a gate, and turn left following Admergill Water once more, now beside a fence, to another stile.

Over the stile, go slightly left to a signpost, and cross the nearby stile, turning right in the ensuing field, following a green path that continues parallel with Admergill Water. Keep following an obvious path until, just after crossing a bridge, it rises to meet a lane.

Turn right for a few strides, then leave the lane, on the left at a wall gap, down steps to a gate into woodland. Follow the on-going path, but on emerging from the trees, leave the path and head across a field to a signpost at a wall end. Cross a through stile here and follow the on-going path, and having crossed a stile, press on along a grassy path across an elongated meadow to meet another lane. At the lane, Blacko Bar Road, turn right for 150yds/m and then leave it on the left, just past the first buildings, at a gap stile. Over the stile the on-going right of way is overgrown and impassable, so immediately cross another stile on the right and then go left alongside a fence to a stile beside a metal gate.

Go forward in the ensuing field alongside a fence and an old hedgerow of beech, hawthorn and holly. The path continues to run on beside a wall, crossing a stile to reach an open pasture. Keep on in the same direction and in the next field follow the path down to join Pendle Water near its confluence with Blacko Water. Cross a footbridge on the left spanning Blacko Water and then go forward following the course of the stream to the confluence. Keep forward until you can cross Pendle Water at a substantial bridge.

Immediately over the bridge turn left on a path between Pendle Water and a fence. Keep on past Old Oak Tree Cottage and a disused weir. When you meet the first

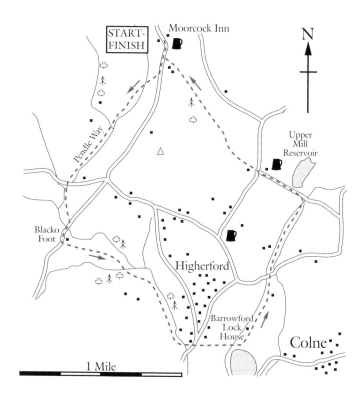

houses on the edge of Higherford go forward on a surfaced lane into Barleydale Road. As you reach an old stone bridge on the left, near the church, go over it and along a cobbled lane to meet the A682. Turn left, and cross the road.

After about 150yds/m branch right on Barnoldswick Road, and 70yds/m further on turn right into Francis Avenue, and when this forks branch right, passing houses and go forward past the last house to an iron kissing gate. Through the gate branch right following a path beside a wall to reach the Leeds and Liverpool Canal at Barrowford Locks and Reservoir. Cross the canal by a bridge and turn left along the towpath.

At Blakey Bridge (No. 144) keep along the towpath, and under bridge 145. At the next bridge the canal goes into the Foulridge Tunnel. Cross the bridge on a rough track and keep on to reach a lane. Turn left and up the lane. After 100yds/m leave it on the left on a signposted footpath over a stile. In the ensuing field bear right, following a fence up-field to a waymark on a fence near a barn conversion.

Go left with the fence, and into the next field. Turn right along a fenceline to a step stile a few strides further on. Cross this and continue, following the line of a fence, to the top of the field and a fence junction, close by which a step stile gives access to the following field. Go up the next field, still with a fence on your right.

In the top corner a stile and wall gap bring you on to a road. The road is busy, and you reach it at a blind bend, so take great care here, and listen for approaching traffic. Keep children and animals under close control.

Cross the road and go up a footpath immediately to the right of a cottage and across its gable end to a step stile. Keep on along a narrow grassy trod across the ensuing field, slightly left, aiming for a through stile in a wall. Over the stile turn right and follow a grassy path beside the wall for 70yds/m, and then, as you pass the end of a line of established holly trees, branch half left across the ensuing field to a wall. Do not cross the wall, but on reaching the wall turn right, following it slightly uphill.

To the left at this point are the buildings of Malkin Tower Farm. This is said to have been a hide-out for Old Mother Demdike, one of the infamous Pendle witches tried in Lancaster in 1612, though others, with some reason, suggest that Blacko Tower is built on the site of Malkin Tower.

When the wall ends you descend towards an overgrown stream. Go left through a gap stile; cross the stream and go forward onto rising ground to locate the remains of an old hawthorn hedgerow. Keep on in the same direction to a wall corner about 150yds/m away.

Now follow the on-going wall up-field to a stile over a fence. Go forward along the ensuing fence to a through stile in a wall. Over the stile turn right for about 50yds/m and then bear left across the field, heading for a gate. Just to the right of the gate, cross the wall by a through stile, and now, with the Moorcock Inn in view, head down to the farm buildings at Admergill Pasture. Another through stile takes you across a wall just behind the farm. Walk past the farm and turn right down its surfaced access lane to reach the main road 100yds/m from the Moorcock Inn.

THE HERDERS INN

*A*n ancient settlement once popular with the Brontë sisters features in this circular walk on the eastern edge of Lancashire

DISTANCE:
7 miles (12km)
ALLOW:
2-3 hours
TERRAIN:
Easy moorland and farmland walking, mostly on good paths
MAP:
OS OLM 21
PUBLIC TRANSPORT:
Bus services operate to Laneshaw Bridge and the walk started at Covey Bridge
PARKING: The Herders Inn (but ask permission first)

The Herders Inn stands on the edge of the wild and desolate Lancashire Moor. This isolated inn, officially called the Oldham Arms, was the Herders House long before it became an inn around 1860, and the building dates back for 300 years. It stands on the site of two herders' cottages. The inn happily caters for walkers, children and dogs (under control), and offers a wide selection of food and drinks. Vegetarians are catered for. Meals are served Monday-Friday 11.30am to 3.00pm and 7.00pm to 11.00pm; Saturday 11.30am to 11.00pm; Sunday 12 noon to 10.30pm. Tel 01282 863443.

The walk begins from the Herders Inn, which boasts an 18th-century facade and which featured in a number of Halliwell Sutcliffe's novels. Before it became an inn the families that lived here – the Laycocks and the Hopkinsons – were involved in handloom weaving. In the early part of the 20th century it was described by an anonymous traveller as "Quite innocent of all modern innovation [with] its clean white wooden benches, and its tidily sanded floor, while its *fare is just as characteristically plain and hearty. A basin of broth, with its toothsome dumpling, for the winter time; the pop and beer 'smiler' for the dog days."*

At the far side of the car park go through a gate and across a small enclosure to another gate, then go forward down a field edge to meet a wall. Turn left beside the wall and descend to cross it at a through stile. On the other side turn right and climb alongside the wall on a narrow grassy path that leads above Foster's Leap.

Foster's Leap is a deep gap between two boulders across which the luckless Foster, caught red-handed rustling sheep, was required to leap if he was to be spared his life. The gap is nothing that would trouble modern athletes, but Foster played safe and tackled the leap on horseback. On landing the horse lost its footing and both horse and rider plunged to their deaths on the rocks below.

Stay close by the wall until, as it bears away to the right, you can go forward on a descending path to cross a surfaced farm access. Go forward beside a wall to a ladder stile. Over the stile keep forward for 30yds/m to a wall corner, and then go half left on a descending path (waymark). At the next waymark, the path forks. Take the less pronounced path descending left, and then go forward through a couple of vaccary walls, then roughly parallel with a fence to reach a stile at a wall gap.

Vaccary walls, erect stone slabs, are the remains of the first farms in this area, and were probably built between the

12th and 15th centuries. Vaccaries were the earliest commercial cattle farms, and first appeared in Lancashire in the Royal Forests such as Trawden.

Go forward across the ensuing field to a gate/stile, at which you reach an ancient trackway. Cross the track to another stile and across the ensuing field to the remains of a wall and an ancient gatepost. Then keep on to another gatepost in midfield. Then a third gatepost before going down to a ladder stile at the bottom of the field that gives on to a track that winds right and left as it leads down into Wycoller village.

Immediately on reaching the village lane go forward to cross a stream, then turn right along the Pendle Way (signposted to Laneshaw Bridge). The lane soon deteriorates into a track between walls. As you reach the entrance to the Old Pump House leave the track over a stile on the left, and keep forward on the ensuing path. Beyond a kissing gate the on-going path is flagged for a short distance, running beside a wall, and then, when it meets a wall, turn left, still on the Pendle Way. At the next waymark cross another stile, and shortly a small footbridge over a stream, then setting off on a broad grassy path across a field. The path soon joins the course of Colne Water, for a short distance before striking across a field to a gate, where it encounters Colne Water once more before running on to meet a road at a kissing gate.

Cross the road and go through a narrow gap stile. (Anyone starting the walk at Laneshaw Bridge will begin at this point.) Over a footbridge take to a crazy-paving path which leads on towards another bridge. Cross this, too, and go up the paved pathway beyond, eventually to emerge into a large open meadow.

Follow the grassy path that swings round to the right to a kissing gate. Beyond this a cinder track runs on, past a recreation area and the Ball Grove Picnic Area. Keep forward past a small lake and then on along a cobbled surface, past a children's play area and a car park to reach a road at Winewall.

Turn left over Colne Water and go past the Cotton Tree pub, and up Winewall Lane. Turn left into Lane Top, and keep going past Hill Top Farm and some disused quarries, continuing across the high point of the lane, and then descending gently. At a second lane junction turn left for 300yds/m until you can leave the lane on an access track leading to Thorn Edge farms. Follow a clear track beyond the farms to meet a crosspath at spot height

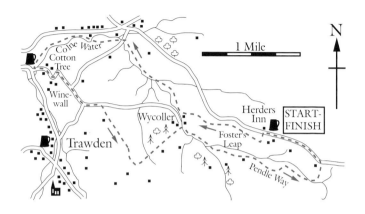

273. Here turn left and descend past Raven's Rock Farm into the village of Wycoller. Continue along the on-going track with the remains of Wycoller Hall on your left. Keep on past the barn on a broad track beside the stream, along the way passing the clam bridge, near a ford.

As you reach the driveway to Dean House Farm branch left on a signposted track (byway to Haworth), continuing now with a stream on your left. As you reach Parson Lee Farm, leave the access track on a narrow path, descending left, and signposted Brontë Way. The narrow path crosses a stile and continues for a short while, broadening out as it rises gently onto open moorland. Follow the track as far as a gate and there cross an adjacent stile onto a vehicle track. Turn left, now leaving the Pendle Way, and continuing with the Brontë Way.

The track swings right, and then heads forward, crosses a stream, and climbs to reach Lancashire Moor Road at a gate. Turn left, and follow the road to the Herders Inn.

Other Dalesman titles for walkers
Pub and Tea Shop Walks Series
LAKE DISTRICT PUB WALKS Terry Marsh £5.99
LAKE DISTRICT TEA SHOP WALKS Mary Welsh £5.99
NORTH YORK MOORS PUB WALKS Richard Musgrave £5.99
PEAK DISTRICT PUB WALKS John Morrison £5.99
YORKSHIRE DALES TEA SHOP WALKS Richard Musgrave £5.95

Walks Around Series: Peak District
BAKEWELL Martin Smith £1.99
BUXTON Andrew McCloy £1.99
CASTLETON John Gillham £1.99
MATLOCK Martin Smith £1.99

Walks Around Series: Lake District
AMBLESIDE Tom Bowker £1.99
HAWKSHEAD Mary Welsh £1.99
KESWICK Dawn Gibson £1.99
WINDERMERE Robert Gambles £1.99

Walking and Trail Guides
LAKE DISTRICT, WESTERN FELLS Paddy Dillon £5.99
LAKE DISTRICT, EASTERN FELLS Paddy Dillon £5.99
WHITE PEAK Martin Smith £4.99
DARK PEAK John Gillham £4.99
NORTH PENNINES Alan Hall £4.99
SOUTH PENNINES John Gillham £4.99
LANCASHIRE John Gillham £4.99
NORTH YORK MOORS Nick Channer £4.99
CLEVELAND WAY Martin Collins £4.99
PENNINE WAY Terry Marsh £4.99
COAST TO COAST Ronald Turnbull £4.99

Safety for Walkers
MOUNTAIN SAFETY Kevin Walker £4.99
MAP READING Robert Matkin £3.50

Available from all good bookshops.
In case of difficulty contact Dalesman Publishing Company,
Stable Courtyard, Broughton Hall, Skipton, North Yorkshire
BD23 3AZ. Tel: 01756 701381